# 100
## YEARS of the
# DETROIT
## HISTORICAL
# SOCIETY

# 100 YEARS of the DETROIT HISTORICAL SOCIETY

 JOEL STONE

WAYNE STATE UNIVERSITY PRESS
*Detroit*

ISBN 978-0-8143-4887-1 (paperback)
ISBN 978-0-8143-4888-8 (ebook)

LIBRARY OF CONGRESS CONTROL NUMBER: 2021932181

Cover design by Katrina Noble

All images in this book are from the Detroit Historical
Society Collection unless otherwise noted.

The three facilities managed by the Detroit Historical Society
rest on land that has been the ancestral homeland of Native Americans
for thousands of years. The sovereign lands to the north and west
of the strait now called the Detroit River were ceded by the
Ojibwe, Odawa, Potawatomi, and Wyandot nations to the United
States through the Treaty of Detroit in 1807. The Detroit
Historical Society affirms Indigenous sovereignty and honors all
tribes and individuals with a connection to Detroit. With our
Native neighbors, the Society can advance educational equity
and promote a better future for the earth and all people.

Wayne State University Press
Leonard N. Simons Building
4809 Woodward Avenue
Detroit, Michigan 48201–1309

Visit us online at wsupress.wayne.edu

This book is dedicated to the people and organizations
that have sustained the Detroit Historical Society through its
first century and are committed to its continued success.

# CONTENTS

Letter from Detroit Historical Society President   9

Letter from Detroit Historical Society Chairperson   11

List of Board of Trustees and Committees   13

List of Current Staff   15

Abbreviations   17

Preface   19

Introduction   21


CHAPTER ONE
The Early Years   27

CHAPTER TWO
Dynamic Growth in a Dynamic City   41

CHAPTER THREE
Driving toward a New Millennium   73

CHAPTER FOUR
Back in the Driver's Seat   99


Appendixes
  A. PAST PRESIDENTS AND LEADERS   107
  B. DETROIT HISTORICAL SOCIETY BALL LOCATIONS   109
  C. CASS LECTURESHIP SERIES   110
  D. HISTORY OF MAJOR SUPPORT GROUPS   111

Acknowledgments   135

Index   137

I am so proud to be introducing *100 Years of the Detroit Historical Society*.

It illuminates our organization's past and helps guide us through our present and on to our future. This rather succinctly defines what we do at the Detroit Historical Society and have done for a century.

We tell the stories of Detroiters and encourage everyone to understand why these stories matter. All of them. There are millions of stories that make this region what it is, and each one is important.

For 100 years, the Society has encouraged historical scholarship, preservation, and education. In partnership with the City of Detroit and generations of sponsors, donors, staff, volunteers, and members, we hold those stories dear. They are captured in a significant collection of artifacts and documents and disseminated through exhibitions, programs, tours, publications, and online content.

This institution has grown and adapted for ten decades and will continue to lead even as the region's cultural needs shift. What Detroiters created here over the last century is amazing. Our challenge is to set the next century up for success so that the Society can continue being Detroit's storyteller.

I speak for all of the directors and staff that came before us when I say that is our commitment every day, recorded here for you to enjoy.

Elana Rugh

As president of the Detroit Historical Society's Board of Trustees, I am humbled by the long line of board leaders who have preceded me and set the Society up for this centenary celebration. The story of their successes is captured in this book and provides an excellent road map for where we've been and where we might be headed.

Besides past Society presidents, I must thank the hundreds of board members who have been so generous with their valuable time, knowledge, and resources, as well as the thousands of volunteers for leading educational tours, serving at events, and processing artifacts. Without ten decades of such commitments, our historical community would be much reduced.

Finally, thank you to the people of Detroit and the communities of southeastern Michigan. You and your ancestors—whether born here or not—made Detroit the city that it is today. Without you, we would have no story to tell. Your interest in this story ensures that future generations will come to understand their rich heritage.

Thank you for supporting our mission.

John Decker

# BOARD OF TRUSTEES AND COMMITTEES

# CURRENT STAFF

Tia Allen
Dontez Bass
Casie Blovsky
Bree Boettner
Leah Buhagiar
Leah Burton
Gail Busby
Kayla Chenault
Toni Cooper
Marcus Craig
Douglas Czajkowski
Eric Dalton
Jeremy Dimick
John Donnelly
Renea Dooley
Kayla Draper
Amanda Ford
Danail Gantchev
Kevin Gramlich
Matthew Greenough
Kevin Hawthorne
Tracy Irwin
Adam Jakubik
Achsha Jones
Ashley Jones
Stevie Jones
Michael Kucharski
Sheena Law-Killinger
Kimberly Luther

Kelsey Mckoy
Patrick Moss
Steven Mrozek
Sarah Murphy
Dean Nasreddine
Gary North
Natalie Pantelis
Lorraine Peake
Sandra Petrey
William Pringle
Malika Pryor
Natalie Renko
Brendan Roney
Elana Rugh
Rebecca Salminen-Witt
Allison Savoy
Brian Schamber
David Schneider
Joel Stone
Rita Taub
Marie Taylor
Delisha Upshaw
Kelli Van Buren
Catherine Waldecker
William Wall-Winkel
Daniel Weed
Justin Williams
David Wilson

# ABBREVIATIONS

| | |
|---|---|
| AAM | American Association of Museums/American Alliance of Museums |
| AASLH | American Association for State and Local History |
| City | City of Detroit, the municipal entity |
| DAR | Daughters of the American Revolution |
| DGLM | Dossin Great Lakes Museum |
| DHM | Detroit Historical Museum |
| DHS | Detroit Historical Society |
| DIA | Detroit Institute of Arts |
| DPL | Detroit Public Library |
| GLMI | Great Lakes Maritime Institute |
| HSM | Historical Society of Michigan |
| ISMA | International Shipmasters Association |
| MHSD | Marine Historical Society of Detroit |
| Wright | Charles H. Wright Museum of African American History |

# PREFACE

THIS book celebrates the Detroit Historical Society and that collective goal of historians, archivists, fundraisers, educators, and volunteers to excite everyone about our city's past. Those who came before showed us many roads to success and how to make Detroit a better place in which to live and work. The Society's responsibility is to capture those lessons and make them available so that anyone can analyze them, learn from them, and use them to create a richer future.

At the Society's first organizational session, the chairman of the meeting, Divie Duffield, threw down the gauntlet. In his opinion, "If the proposed society could not do something worthwhile, it would be unwise to attempt to do anything at all." In today's parlance, "Go big or go home." This volume should satisfy everyone that something worthwhile was accomplished and continues to grow, but Mr. Duffield's caution remains valid.

If we are trusted, that trust must be respected. If we want to excite our community, our offerings need to reflect that community. If we want people to invest, there must be a tangible benefit—idealistic or physical—to that request. The Detroit Historical Society has established itself as a respectful, yet aggressive, agile, and imaginative player in the public history world and should remain so. This is a suitable challenge for us and our successors that really hasn't changed much in a hundred years.

Most established institutions, from families to municipalities, find foundation in their history and strength in the original documents that define that history. In Detroit, an impressive archival collection was assembled by Clarence Burton that focused primarily on early Detroit. He donated his collection to the Detroit Public Library in 1915, and it soon became a highlight of the new building on Woodward Avenue in 1921. It is here that the Detroit Historical Society began.

Like siblings, the Burton Historical Collection and the Society have grown together: close in their youth, increasingly independent as they matured, but still united by a shared heritage and mission. The Society's family also includes two municipal entities—the Detroit Historical Commission and the Detroit Historical Department—as well as innumerable internal support groups, volunteers, and external partners. This volume will endeavor to weave these all into a broad narrative illustrating the fortunes of this important and enduring cultural institution.

Records of the early Detroit Historical Society—referred to throughout this volume as the Society or DHS—were kept by Burton Historical Collection chief Miss Gracie Krum. It is fortunate that she wrote a history of the Society in 1952 based on those notes, because most of the early records have gone missing. It is an unfortunate truth that historical organizations often preserve their own histories least. Research for this publication relied on various printed materials created by the Society, as well as interviews, newspapers, and other primary sources.

# INTRODUCTION

PEOPLE have lived in the region around the strait now called the Detroit River for thousands of years. Evidence of permanent habitation dates to 800–1,000 years ago. Gradual infiltration of western Europeans started in the 1600s and became a permanent feature in 1701, making Detroit one of the older European settlements in North America.

Thus, by the time 1921 rolled around, the city already had centuries of history under its belt. A number of civic-minded leaders recognized that capturing our past should be a priority, and the Detroit Historical Society was born.

Over a century, it has grown from a small semi-professional fraternity that offered talks and lectures into one of the respected metropolitan public history organizations in the nation. Documenting that journey has revealed numerous instances of hard lessons learned and over-the-top successes. This volume is meant to touch on all of those with appropriate empathy.

The journey of this Society over the last century also provides a reflective road map of the route that museums around the world have taken to understand and address their stewardship of the past, place in the present, and responsibilities to the future. In this regard, Detroit was both a leader and—unintentionally—a laggard. The Michigan Historical Society (today the Historical Society of Michigan) was founded in 1828, before Michigan Territory became a state, and was based in Detroit. It was the seventh such organization in the United States and the earliest outside of the original thirteen colonies. It remains Michigan's oldest cultural organization.

For many years, the Michigan society served as the historical voice in Detroit, even as other cities in the Midwest created local historical societies before and after the American Civil War. When Detroit launched its historical society in 1921, the Cincinnati Historical Society was already three-quarters of a century old. The founders recognized that their new organization was significantly behind its neighbors, but that did not last long. Within thirty years, the Detroit Historical Society boasted the largest membership of any local history organization in the nation. In 1964, Henry Brown, managing director of the Historical Department and coordinating director of the Society, became president of the American Association for State and Local History, the largest organization for historical museums and museum professionals in North America.

The post–World War II period saw a new public-private business model develop in Detroit, a model that proved successful for half a century and was copied elsewhere. The DHS partnered with the City to create the Detroit Historical Commission and the Detroit Historical Department, which built and managed the museums and collections facilities that are still part of our historical equation. Additionally, the Society developed relationships with internal and external affinity groups and volunteer organizations that proved invaluable in advancing the overall historical dialogue in the region.

This fine model was not impervious to the changing fortunes in the city it represented nor to the politics that can be found in such intermingled relationships. After fifty years, a new model returned most aspects of daily operations to the Detroit Historical Society, with financial and facility support provided by the City of Detroit. Once again, these changes reflected patterns and challenges that were being experienced in museums and public history organizations around the world. And once again, after fifteen additional years of reacting to a rapidly changing social and economic landscape, the Detroit Historical Society emerged a recognized leader.

And therein lies the challenge. Can we do it for another century? Nationwide, according to the American Alliance of Museums, historical museums and sites represent about 50 percent of cultural facilities—art museums, science museums, zoos, aquariums, and so forth—and are among the most trusted institutions in our communities. Yet history generally comes last in terms of attendance and donated revenues.

There are a number of reasons for the disparity, but the fact remains that there is passion in our community for capturing and preserving material culture and telling Detroit's many stories. Satisfying that passion remains the same challenge that was addressed in the Detroit Public Library's Club Room a hundred years ago.


### DETROIT IN 1921

Nineteen twenty-one was the year that a small number of influential Detroiters decided to start another "club" in a town already full of clubs. To them it seemed an opportune time to promote such an endeavor. Despite an economic downturn following the disruption of World War I and the Spanish flu epidemic, what had been a second-tier foundry town was blossoming. Actually, exploding

Photograph of Cadillac Square about 1919 looking toward City Hall. Within a few years, Barlum Tower would rise in the first block on the right.

might be more accurate. In 1900, Detroit ranked thirteenth among American cities in population. By 1920, it had risen to fourth.

In the late nineteenth century, Detroit became a leader in copper, brass, iron, and steel production. Its advantageous location on the Great Lakes allowed for easy access to the ores and limestone of the north country and the coal of Ohio and Pennsylvania; the Detroit River carried more tonnage than any waterway in the world. As a result, more railcars and iron stoves were made in Detroit than anywhere else on the continent. Shipbuilding companies along the St. Clair and Detroit rivers turned out more vessels than anywhere else on the Lakes, and the city boasted the largest facilities for rolling, extruding, and pouring copper and brass.

Beyond commercial metallurgy, Detroit led the nation in pharmaceutical development and supported several chemical, paint, and refining operations. Printing was also big business, with names like Calvert, Polk, Remick, and the Detroit Photographic Company producing advertising, directories, sheet music, and color postcards for wide distribution. S. S. Kresge, Ferry Seeds, and later Burroughs, Eureka, Frigidaire, Kelvinator, and Chris-Craft were national brands based in the Detroit area. Other world-class factories made furniture, pianos and organs, shoes and boots, and cigars.

This healthy economic diversity was undermined by the growing popularity of automobiles. While not invented here, by 1915 Detroit led the world in automobile manufacturing with over forty companies making cars and seventy-plus supplying the industry. Good wages in the auto plants had two significant impacts: they made it harder for smaller industries to compete for workers, and they drew job seekers from Europe and the American South.

Detroit has always been home to migrating populations. The Native populations were transient prior to the influx of Europeans; the tribes here in 1500 CE were not the same ones here in 1600. Once in American hands, the city became home to many German and Irish immigrants prior to 1850. In the second half of the century, those populations continued to grow, joined by Polish, Canadian (mostly English and Scot), Italian, Belgian, Lebanese, Serbian, Hungarian, and Russian émigrés. In 1910, most Detroiters were foreign-born or first-generation citizens who lived in roughly homogeneous neighborhoods that reflected the cultural norms of their residents. A significant number of the working class were educated and highly skilled tradesmen. A significant portion of the new folks were Catholic—either Roman or Orthodox—challenging the Protestant hierarchy. Detroit's Jewish population also expanded significantly, and the city got its first Muslim mosque.

The burst of American-born migration into the city riled this melting pot. Poor Whites from Appalachia and Black farmers of modest means from the extreme southern states were thrust into a town that was short on housing, and neither group was particularly welcome. Job postings that used to say "Irish Need Not Apply" now said "No Hillbillies" and "No Negroes" or "No Coloreds." And in the end, it was all about the jobs. Detroit had them but was overwhelmed by the flood of hardworking people who wanted them.

Between 1900 and 1918, Detroit's footprint grew from 36 square miles to 76. After that, it almost doubled to over 138 square miles by 1926, its current size. Neighborhoods close to the city center were being repurposed for larger commercial sites, and new residential spaces were being created. During the 1920s, Detroit put in more infrastructure than any city its size in the country.

During the second decade of the twentieth century, significant construction was underway. Several downtown buildings joined the Majestic and Dime Bank buildings in the "skyscraper" category. Slightly outside of the city center, a new train station rose eighteen stories over Corktown, and Orchestra Hall, opened in 1919 on Woodward, soon proved itself one of the most acoustically perfect concert venues in the world. The *Detroit News* and *Detroit Free Press* got new Albert Kahn–designed headquarters. Several new hospitals were opened, including Henry Ford, Women's (later renamed Hutzel), and—way out in the country—Herman Kiefer. As a precursor to the influence the automobile would have on all aspects of Detroit culture, concrete was first used to pave a stretch of Woodward Avenue in 1909 and gradually was used to create hundreds of miles of new roads. Concrete, reinforced with steel, also became the product of choice for building most new auto plants.

Besides automobiles, other technologies were taking off. By 1910, telephones and electric lighting had become common. In 1911, members of the Country Club of Detroit out in cottage country—Grosse Pointe—brought a Wright Brothers airplane to the golf course for three days of demonstration flights. They ended up purchasing the marvel. Thomas Clark had placed wireless telegraphs on several Detroit & Cleveland Navigation Co. vessels and later ship-to-shore radio—a Great Lakes first. Clark would also influence William Scripps's project to put the first schedule of commercial programming on a radio station. WWJ (then 8MK) went live in 1920. Detroit's thriving live theater scene was quickly shifting to movies and soon claimed one of the largest theater districts in the country.

From a social standpoint, Michigan approved a statewide alcohol prohibition law in 1916 that went into effect in 1918. This had been a popular cause among religious conservatives for nearly a century and remained popular in the state's rural areas. However, Detroit's diverse, blue-collar immigrant population—with German, Polish, and Irish majorities—quickly found ways to skirt the law. The statute was overturned on a technicality in 1919 but offered a foreshadowing of disruptions and political stances that would reappear with nationwide Prohibition in 1920.

Social clubs were mentioned earlier, and Detroit had them: sports, music, theater, literary, religious, educational, patriotic. It would do a disservice to this narrative to not mention some of them—many of which are still active today—because they reflect how adults prioritized their free time in the days before radio and television. While most are now represented by a broad and diverse membership, that wasn't always the case. In fact, groups with men-only or women-only admission were the norm. Jews and Blacks were generally not welcome, unless it was a Jewish or Negro club. Several of the largest clubs were ethnically focused and viewed outsiders with suspicion, particularly when wars raged in Europe.

During the 1910s, the Prismatic Club, among the oldest all-male literary clubs in the country (1867), was moving into a new home in the Brush Park neighborhood. A similar organization for women, formed in 1873, eventually became the politically active Twentieth Century Club. The Fine Arts Society of Detroit (1906), Theater Arts Club of Detroit (1910), an all-female troupe, and Players (1911), a male theatrical club, all provided amateur theater. In 1907, graphic artists formalized their organization, changing the name from the Hopkin Club to the Scarab Club. Amateur musical groups were legion. Nearly every large company had a band and every church a choir. Ethnic groups like the St. Andrews Society (1849), German Harmonie Club (1852), eastside Dom Polksi (1912), and Gaelic League (1920) promoted music, some in impressive clubhouses.

Community support organizations took off in the 1910s, created to address urban issues that accompanied intense industrialization and mass migration. Businessmen formed two clubs that would soon expand nationally and a third that became a local Christmas tradition: National Exchange Club in 1911, Goodfellows/Old Newsboys in 1914, and Kiwanis in 1915. White women's clubs came together under the banner of the Women's City Club in 1919. Black organizations with a national presence formed local chapters and included the National Association for the Advancement of Colored People (NAACP) in 1912 and the Detroit Urban League in 1916. Women within the African American community joined forces in 1898 to launch the Detroit Study Club, which supported the Phillis Wheatley Home for Aged Colored Ladies and numerous other programs.

Sports clubs in Detroit were as ubiquitous as music clubs and often shared membership. There was a succession of active rowing clubs dating to 1839. In addition to the Detroit Boat Club and Detroit Yacht Club, sporting beautiful new clubhouses, the Edison Boat Club (1914) and Bayview Yacht Club (1915) established a competitive sailboat racing community. Speedboat racing was catching on but was truly a sport of the wealthy. Baseball, bowling, and bicycling were well established by 1920. Corporate clubs joined stand-alone clubs at competitions generally under the auspices of the Amateur Athletic Union. The Wolverine Wheelsmen (Wolverine Sports Club in 2020), established in 1888, operated out of a beautiful clubhouse on Adams Street. The Detroit Athletic Club, established in 1887, found new life in 1913 and opened a grand new clubhouse in 1915.

Into this milieu the Detroit Historical Society was born. The narrative that follows shows that the original mission was always presumed to be more professional than social. Etymology suggests that a society is a social organization—informally a club—but Detroit didn't need any more clubs. It needed a champion standing apart from the maelstrom to capture, preserve, and tell the city's story in all its many facets.

# CHAPTER ONE

# THE EARLY YEARS

If the proposed society could not do something worthwhile, it would be unwise to attempt to do anything at all.

—DIVIE DUFFIELD, DHS FOUNDER

O N December 10, 1921, a simple letter was sent to a number of local men. "You are cordially invited to join a little company of Congenial spirits on Thursday evening, December 15, 1921 at 7:45 o'clock in the club room third floor of the new Public Library, Woodward Avenue. The purpose of the meeting is to discuss the advisability of organizing a Detroit Historical Society to work in conjunction with the Burton Historical Collection and the Michigan Historical Society. We will visit the Burton Library. Please do not fail us." The letter was signed by Divie Duffield, Clarence Burton, and Albert Finn.

On the appointed day, they were joined by nine other men and Gracie Krum, the librarian who managed Burton's extensive collection at the Detroit Public Library (DPL). They included Charles D. Cameron, George B. Catlin, Franklin S. Dewey, J. Bell Moran, Charles R. Robertson, John A. Russell, Dr. Rev. Robert J. Service, William Stocking, and Thomas A. E. Weadock. Students of Detroit history will recognize George Catlin, *Detroit News* historian and author, and William Stocking, statistician for the Chamber of Commerce and associate editor of Burton's ubiquitous *History of Detroit, 1701–1922*. J. Bell Moran remained a leader of the newly minted historical society through the 1960s.

Finn, initially serving as Secretary, requested that Miss Krum take notes as secretary and that Duffield, president of the Detroit Library Commission, chair this first meeting. Duffield called the meeting to order and, in Krum's words, "expressed hearty interest in the objects for which it had been called," then offered the cautionary advice that opens this chapter.

A second meeting was held in the Club Room on January 5, 1922, when "President Burton" called the meeting to order, and bylaws drawn up by Finn were approved. Moran was elected treasurer, a position he held for many years. Additional attendees included Rev. G. G. Atkins, Frank Cody, superintendent of Detroit Public Schools (DPS), and Adam Strohm, director of the DPL. Typical for this period, the founders of the Society reflected the leadership in the city: established, upper-class, White businessmen. There would be a gradual diversification of membership, but it was a decades-long process. Gathering in the Club Room was entirely appropriate at the time.

## STRICTLY LITERARY

As described in the initial notice, the Society was launched as a support arm for the DPL and the Burton collection. The fall schedule included a handful of public lectures offered by Burton and W. L. Jenks of Port Huron addressing Detroit's early history to groups that included the Sons of the American Revolution, Daughters of the American Revolution (DAR), students from the Michigan State Normal College (today Eastern Michigan University) in Ypsilanti, and a large group of teachers from the DPS. On April 20, 1922, the DHS held its first "Open Meeting," attended by various historic and patriotic group members and the general public. Carl E. Pray of the Normal College discussed the romantic allure of the French voyageurs. By March, standing committees for research (Divie Duffield), membership (George Canfield), and educational (Rev. Gaius Atkins) initiatives were appointed, and Miss Krum was officially the assistant secretary and representative to the Michigan Historical Society. She noted at this point that "the Society's organization was now complete." True for the moment, but not for long.

After a summer respite, the primary order of business was discussion related to a Society-published monthly newsletter. Burton was so interested that he had printing quotes in hand and offered to cover any deficit that the endeavor might incur. This publication was short-lived, but several decades later publishing became an important part of the Society's mission.

Articles of incorporation were presented in executive session and signed on December 7, 1922, in the Burton stacks, followed by a lecture titled "Cadillac and the Founding of Detroit" by Burton in the DPL Assembly Room. The first Annual Meeting was held on January 10, 1923, in the same space. There was $140.49 cash on hand, all officers were reelected, and a presentation about the Underground Railroad was given by William Siebert of Ohio State University. Jared Finney, son of Underground Railroad activist Seymour Finney, was asked for reminiscences.

For the next several years, the Society's annual calendar was similar. Lectures, roughly monthly, were presented at the DPL, Cass Technical High School, and other appropriate venues. The publication *Detroit Historical Monthly* resulted when Burton decided that he wanted more than a newsletter; the DPL was already publishing the *Burton Historical Leaflet*, edited by Miss Krum. A committee of newspapermen representing the *Michigan Manufacturer*, *Financial Record*, *Detroit News*, and *Detroit Free Press* were appointed to the publication committee. Responsibility for editing and production fell to Miss Krum, with the first edition out in March 1924. In June, Finn resigned as secretary, and Krum was "appointed to assume his duties for the rest of the year."

Gracie Krum remained secretary of the Detroit Historical Society until 1934 and a director emeritus until her death in 1957. When appointed the official steward of Clarence Burton's material at the new library, she embraced the many facets of his vision and extended his legacy for years after he had died. In this capacity, the oft-cited approbation "Godmother of the Detroit Historical Society" is appropriate.

*Detroit Historical Monthly* was suspended after four issues. Despite interest from academic institutions in North America and Europe, response in Detroit was tepid and the scholarship could not justify the costs. The lecture series continued.

### LET THE COLLECTION BEGIN

Interest in local history was very high at this time, generally related to colonial European migration and the settlement's early years. Promotion of the new Detroit Historical Society had one desired result: donations of documents and records to the Burton collection began to increase substantially. There was also an unintended result: people were interested in donating artifacts like furniture, household effects, and personal belongings. As these did not fall within the Burton's archival scope, Society leaders realized that rather than let many valuable artifacts go to auction houses and antique dealers, some accommodation should be found to house these materials.

In Miss Krum's words, "J. Bell Moran sensed this need and he realized too that the Society required an objective of wider appeal than the assembling of documentary materials afforded." The mention of wider appeal is important here, for by 1927 membership in the Society was stagnant. Lectures drew a modest, predictable crowd, but with the deaths of a few of the founding members, the high hopes of previous years were fading.

The new main branch of the Detroit Public Library opened on Woodward Avenue in March 1921.

Clarence Burton's collection of regional documents became a centerpiece of the library's holdings.

Strategies were devised to correct these issues, which by 1931 led to a new management structure, new public offerings, and updated bylaws. In October 1927, addressing the need for space, J. Bell Moran secured a small office on the twenty-third floor of the Barlum Tower on Cadillac Square (today Cadillac Tower). This was to be used to facilitate the clerical work of the Society and serve as artifact storage.

Meanwhile, President Burton secured the services of T. J. Haggerty, who had recently worked to boost membership at the Founders Society of the Detroit Institute of Arts. Dues which had been $2 for active members were raised to $10. Haggerty was to receive 20 percent of each regular membership and 10 percent for higher membership contributions. He was also authorized to "build a staff of solicitors" who would work out of the new office space. Miss C. J. Given was his first hire.

At this juncture, Haggerty hatched a scheme to build membership quickly by merging with an outside organization known as the Gristmill Club. Krum described this organization in loose terms: "A large group of Detroiters who met periodically at dinner to talk of old times." Membership was pegged at about 400 men, and the proposal was that their dues would double to $20, with $10 of that making them active members of the Detroit Historical Society. In the near term, it sounded like a good deal for the Society. In the not very long term, the Gristmill Club saw their membership drop by 75 percent, and the relationship was dissolved by December 1930.

Basic Society membership fees returned to $2. In February 1928, ill health required Haggerty to step away. Miss Given worked with Treasurer Moran to rebuild membership. At an executive session, she requested money to put together a simple membership brochure, but the matter was tabled.

More than anyone, Moran understood that the Society was asking members for money with very little to offer in return. He envisioned a museum where the artifacts that were slowly accumulating should be interpreted for students and scholars. The board started soliciting widely for possible sites. The Detroit Institute of Arts, city-owned space in the Water Board Building downtown, homes in the Midtown neighborhood (including Burton's), the Grand Army of the Republic building, the Whitney home—all were considered.

The temporary answer came in the form of expanded office space in Barlum Tower. Krum wrote, "November 19 [1928] marks the formal beginning of the Detroit Historical Museum," when a single large office space—rooms 2302–18—was rented. Arthur Hampton was hired as the first curator and accepted the first officially accessioned artifact: a short length of tamarack log that was part of Detroit's first frontier water system. Within three years, over 2,500 objects had been accepted.

Located on the twenty-third floor of Barlum Tower, the Detroit Historical Society's "cabinet of curiosities" was billed as the highest museum in the world when it opened in 1928.

## THE HIGHEST MUSEUM IN THE WORLD

The new space near the top of Barlum Tower allowed the Society to expand its public offerings, slowly at first. Initially open only from 3 to 5 p.m., hours were expanded to 1 to 5 p.m. two years later.

The first big event took place on February 9, 1929, when the membership gathered and "the feeling of ownership added much to the spirit of the meeting." Notably, at the Annual Meeting held a month earlier, a quorum of officers and board members was not in attendance. Younger board members deferred to the older members. Despite progress, meeting notes suggest that it was frustratingly slow. Standing committees included research, membership, educational, finance, publicity, and social.

Support for this new museum from sister organizations was strong. Both the Detroit Institute of Arts and the Burton Historical Collection loaned material to help Mr. Hampton with interpretation. The first focused installation was from Hampton's personal collection of lighting instruments: candleholders and oil lamps. The Society later purchased this collection.

While the lectures were held in the more accommodating spaces at the DPL and dinners held in hotels, the museum hosted a broad array of patriotic and civic organizations. Docent volunteers were available for demonstrations on spinning and weaving. Special days were publicized for cobbling, policing, logging, firefighting, and Michigan in the Civil War. Teas were common, and era-oriented fashion shows were organized.

The room became a natural meeting space for Lincoln or Washington birthday celebrations and crafting gatherings, as well as an incubator for ideas, but it wasn't big enough for much else. Even with the addition of a small business office and conference room, the accommodations were tight.

The biggest obstacle to attendance: Who looks for a museum in a skyscraper? After a few years, it became clear that, from a visitor perspective, the Barlum Tower space was untenable. Except perhaps on Coney Island, museums were stand-alone buildings with large display spaces. From a practical perspective, the elevators couldn't handle large groups, and parking was limited. From an archival standpoint, George Catlin, trustee and *Detroit News* historian, cited in Krum's notes as writing the Common Council in August 1933, suggested that a museum should be accessible and free to the public—despite difficult times—and that "its collection of material is steadily growing and its present space is badly crowded."

Certainly, the trustees understood these problems. As early as September 8, 1930, the seeds were planted for the current museum building. Clarence Burton, writing to his old compatriot Divie Duffield, lamented, "There is no large city in the United States that . . . has not a Museum except Detroit." Burton suggested approaching Henry Ford about a parcel of land he owned adjacent to the new library, on the corner of Woodward and Kirby streets.

## SOCIAL INTERCHANGE

While the Society was established by gentlemen, it wasn't long before ladies began to play a significant role in maintaining early momentum. Scholastic lectures remained the main programming, but by April 1924 social meetings started a successful trend that would last through today.

In 1925, a proposal was made to either make the winter Annual Meeting a social affair or create such an event at the end of the "season" in April or May. Nineteen twenty-eight saw new faces on the Board of Trustees, including Mattie (Mrs. Charles H.) Metcalf (also president of the Historic Memorials Society), Miss Myrtle Babcock, and Miss M. Agnes Burton—Clarence Burton's daughter—a librarian and childhood friend of Gracie Krum.

In 1929, the Society worked with the Burton collection to mount a promotional exhibit at the Third Annual Fur Show at Masonic Temple. They focused on John Jacob Astor and the American Fur Company material held in Detroit. Fashion became a popular element of events for many years.

At the Eighth Annual Meeting in January 1930, held at the Central Woodward Christian Church, Krum noted that "the possibility of the organization of a Women's Committee to assist in furthering the work of the Society is under consideration." By late April it was a reality, its stated purpose being to fund an endowment for a stand-alone historical museum.

On May 28, 1931, the Women's Division held its first Annual Meeting at the Women's City Club. The "Old Detroit Committee" was formed to produce a calendar as a fundraising project. By December, they were on sale in Barlum Tower as well as at Hudson's and Kern's department stores. By January, about 300 copies had been sold, realizing a profit of $15.

In the meantime, Gracie Krum contacted member Jessie Bonstelle, dramatist and director of the Bonstelle Civic Theatre, requesting assistance to enliven monthly programming instead of the "quiet old-fashioned way" that is "not attractive to a great many members, and increasingly at variance with modern social habits." Clearly, she was interested in shaking up the stodgy luncheon talks, but though the two met, no obvious changes took place.

With a request for room fees from the library in 1932, monthly gatherings increasingly involved dinners in the private dining rooms of places like the Wardell Hotel (today the Park Shelton) and the Colony Town Club on East Jefferson Avenue. Starting in December 1936, lunchtime meetings became more popular, particularly in the Hotel Statler's newly named Judge Woodward Room, which was made available to the Society free of charge.

Band concerts, commemorations, and dedications were regular entries in meeting minutes, which were assumed by or assigned to the Women's Division. Indeed, Krum writes in late 1932, "It was at this period, that the assistance rendered by the women's patriotic societies was broadened." Various chapters of the DAR and the Historic Memorials Society began making contributions earmarked for museum rent, to weather the Great Depression.

The DHS board never embraced the Women's Division, and frustration among the ladies resulted in a motion at their Annual Meeting on May 31, 1934, to discontinue the group. The motion did not pass but resulted in a suggestion to make the organization simply a standing committee within the DHS. When that notion was proposed at a meeting of trustees on June 11, the board tabled it.

Nineteen months later, on February 1, 1936, a group of seven stalwarts that included Agnes Burton met at Gracie Krum's apartment in the Wardell Hotel across the street from the main library. Krum and Burton were tasked with "requesting" that the status of their group within the Society be defined and recognized so that they could get on with their work.

At a scheduled meeting that evening, held in the Indian Village home of DHS President Orla B. Taylor, to "consider the financial situation of the Society and to transact other necessary business," the "Women's Committee" was accepted and charged with planning all future meeting programming. Agnes Burton was the committee's representative to the board. The Women's Committee appears to have been reimagined as the Detroit Historical Society Guild in 1951.

## THE LEAN YEARS

A number of things happened in the mid-1930s that affected the cohesion and focus of the Society during the darkest years of the Depression. Notable was the November 1932 death of Clarence Burton, Society founder and leading champion of Detroit history. Also significant were ongoing fiscal issues and unproductive strategic initiatives.

In addition to creating the Women's Committee, several male DHS board members promoted a partnership with the Detroit Business Pioneers. Created as a unit of the Detroit Board of Commerce sometime in 1929, the Pioneers were dedicated to "Preserving the Traditions of Old Detroit" and "Promoting the Development of New Detroit." It was hoped that the Society's participation with the Pioneers would help open doors to political and financial support.

One opportunity presented itself when the Pioneers organization launched a new publication in fall 1934 called *Pioneering*. President Howard I. Harvey suggested that the Society make it their official magazine, and DHS President Thomas Weadock accepted his offer. The same offer was accepted by the Burton collection and the Detroit Old Timers' Association.

In May 1935, the Detroit Business Pioneers sponsored an end-of-season "1880's Costume Dinner Ball" at the Dearborn Inn to which Society members were invited. In January 1937, the Pioneers sponsored a similar "Michigan Centennial Costume Cotillion" at the same venue. The relationship between the Pioneers and the Society, in various forms, lasted until the late 1970s.

In September 1935, Curator Arthur Hampton, writing to DHS First Vice President Percival Fitzsimmons, denoted a simple budget where he made $33.17 per month—about $400 per annum, or $18,000 in 2021 dollars. By comparison, an able-bodied seaman on a Great Lakes freighter made about $83 a month, and a good hotel waiter maybe $60.

Hampton's letter to Fitzsimmons inquired about the $16.20 incurred by sending staff to the State Fair with a simple exhibit of weaving and spinning. The cost was paid out of Hampton's pocket, and was modest because one staffer only charged bus fare and the other charged a few lunches. The team collected $5.36 in donations, but those were earmarked for the Replica Project, a newly hatched concept on the horizon.

To accommodate an upcoming exhibit at the Naval Armory, in a space twice as large as the State Fair's, Hampton preyed on the good graces of the Detroit

Fire Department for a truck to collect more material. In response to Hampton's inquiry about increased financial resources, Fitzsimmons quietly complimented his efforts, suggested that increased public contributions were necessary, and noted that parts of Hampton's staff salaries were already being absorbed by board members. He stated that the money must be found elsewhere.

In the meantime, some trustees were avidly pursuing what became known as the Replica Project. Conceptually, this was to be an outdoor history attraction re-creating elements of founding French governor Antoine Laumet de Lamothe Cadillac's Fort Pontchartrain in Gabriel Richard Park near the Belle Isle Bridge. It was also meant to be the Society's new home and have exhibition space, offices, and collections storage. With a nod to longevity, the fort and buildings were to be built of molded concrete logs and include an adjoining reimagined Native American village. The idea attracted some big names, including one of the deans of Detroit architecture, George Mason, Diocese of Detroit historian Rev. George Paré, and City Councilman Eugene Van Antwerp. Notably, the 1936 Annual Meeting focused on the project, and reports related to the museum and membership were omitted.

Admittedly, the museum was not paying for itself, and outreach efforts were authentically interactive yet humble. In the minds of the board, the Replica Project was an opportunity to take Detroit's historical narrative to a higher level. The fact that membership was neglected on the Annual Meeting agenda represents a problem left unaddressed. Early on, Krum announced membership numbers in her notes. Those figures soon went unrecorded.

Board members visited numerous churches and ethnic societies to promote the fort. At the end of April, the Society sent out direct inquiries to a number of patriotic organizations regarding their interest in providing funding for the Replica Project. The sixteen responses they received were generally supportive but lacked any financial commitment. After many months, and with only about $15 in the dedicated account, the trustees deemed it "advisable to abandon the project." This was a blow.

A real boost came when President Orla Taylor and Treasurer Moran were able to get the Detroit Arts Commission to commit $1,500 to the museum for fiscal year 1937–38. At this point, annual revenues were split evenly to pay rent and Hampton's salary, minus $120 for operating expenses. This represented a significant pay increase for the curator. The commitment of the Arts Commission was confirmed for a second year. Additionally, the Tracy McGregor Fund dedicated $100 annually over five years for the curator's salary. In an interesting snapshot of Hampton's newfound status, he undertook a quick professional visit to New York City museums, met a number of other curators, and in the second year of the McGregor grant suggested that the money might be better used to purchase a collection of photographs of historic Michigan logging operations.

Foreshadowing events a decade later, members of the Society were invited to visit the schooner *J. T. Wing* at her berth near Waterworks Park (officially Gladwin Park). The vessel was the last working sail craft on the Great Lakes, and ownership had recently passed from Braun Lumber to the established ship chandlery firm owned by Jefferson Thurber Wing. As suggested in Krum's notes, it was a unique opportunity. Coincidentally, a month later, in May 1937, the Society went on record urging preservation of the historic buildings at Fort Wayne in Springwells. Both the *Wing* and the fort would play significant roles in the Society's future.

As 1939 opened, another bit of serendipity occurred when George Stark of the *Detroit News*, Raymond Miller and Joe Norris from Wayne University (which became Wayne State University in 1956), and F. Clever Bald of the Detroit Institute of Technology all were slated as speakers for the Society's spring lectures. These men would also play significant roles in the Society's future.

The topic of a permanent home for the museum came up often in trustee meetings. Wayne University was approached but demurred. President Taylor engaged the Rackham Fund, but despite an initially positive reaction he was ultimately disappointed. The Hecker family declined its Woodward property, and the DuCharme Home on Jefferson was deemed too close to the river's foundry district.

## CHANGES IN THE HISTORICAL LANDSCAPE

Several important steps were taken at this time toward a more professional organization. First, Women's Committee member Florence Marsh, coauthor of the recently published *History of Detroit for Young People*, took over as membership chair and launched a new Saturday series of "Reminiscence" meetings at the DPL Assembly Room. Based on her experience with the Detroit Society for Genealogical Research, formed in 1936, she felt that midweek luncheon meetings excluded a large number of potential members. At this time, annual dues were still only $2 for a basic membership.

Additionally, the Society joined the Conference of Historical Societies, which had been founded in 1904. Gracie Krum attended its conference in Washington, D.C., and was part of discussions that resulted in an organizational name change in 1940 to the American Association for State and Local History (AASLH). The Detroit Historical Society has been an active member of AASLH ever since.

Staff was involved in the Michigan History Conference that took place at Wayne University in May 1940, and Arthur Hampton was a speaker at the 35th

Annual Meeting of the American Association of Museums (today the American Alliance of Museums, or AAM), which took place in Detroit that year. The DHS became a member of AAM that year and remains so.

Heading into the 1940s, the Society settled into a routine. The museum hosted talks and lectures on Saturday afternoons and introduced Hobby Days where members of specific affinity groups gathered to display buttons, stamps, currency, historic glass, dolls—objects that grab people's interest. The facility was popular with school groups, although the management of Barlum Tower grew increasingly frustrated with large groups commandeering the elevators. DHS members participated in outside activities like Lincoln and Washington birthday celebrations, Armistice Day commemorations, and significant anniversary events.

In August 1940, Julia Hubbard, a DHS trustee and Wayne University faculty member, launched the Society's first youth program. One of its stated goals was "to promote an opportunity for young people from various walks of life to meet in an informal social spirit for the discussion of problems vital to city life . . . in connection with the future development of their city." Trustees approved the addition of the "Junior Group" in a special meeting on September 20. Designed for teens, it focused on high school juniors and seniors.

While progress was being made, 1940 was the first year since its opening that the museum did not throw itself a birthday party on November 19. Additionally, in a beautifully worded note to Adam Strohm, head librarian at the DPL, Miss Krum—both head of the Burton collection under Strohm and secretary for the DHS—wrote, "At the last meeting of the Trustees of the Detroit Historical Society, Mr. Harold M. Hastings and Mr. Thomas I. Starr were appointed a committee to formulate plans for carrying forward the secretarial work of the Society which has heretofore centered in the Burton Historical Collection." After eighteen years, the bond between the library and the Society—always polite and professional—was getting thinner.

In January 1942, Arthur Hampton presented a very complete accounting of activity for his organization—the first time that Krum included such a report in her narrative. The federal Works Progress Administration paid the salaries of people to inventory the 9,955 archived objects—the Society's first collections inventory. The museum hosted 24 adult groups and 94 school groups, totaling 6,830 visitors. Hampton had developed good relations with the regional school systems and the Detroit Board of Education, as well as the local court officers that sent jury folk—perhaps during a recess—to the museum. The newspapers, particularly the *Detroit News*, helped publicize its events and solicit donations to the collection. Hampton specifically thanked the City, the DIA, and the Burton Historical Collection for their "many courtesies." Soon afterward, he took a medical leave, and while he returned for a few days in June, his tenure was finished. In retrospect, his letter has the tenor of a farewell. He died on Lincoln's birthday in 1943.

About this time, Krum was retiring from her responsibilities as chief at the Burton Historical Collection. Mabel (Mrs. Lloyd DeWitt) Smith, a trustee, assumed duties as recording secretary of the Society. Louisa Butler, assistant curator, assumed responsibilities for museum activities.

In 1940, J. Bell Moran became president of the Detroit Historical Society. He had been an active force within the Society since its inception. However, in June 1942, about the same time that Hampton left for good and the museum closed for several months, Moran was commissioned into the United States Army and resigned his position with the Society.

At a special meeting of the trustees on July 12, Thomas Starr nominated George Stark to become president. Seconded by Rabbi Dr. Leo Franklin, that motion was approved. A new era was about to unfold for the Society.

# CHAPTER TWO

# DYNAMIC GROWTH IN A DYNAMIC CITY

It is regrettable, but it is true, that the town having the richest
tradition and the most colorful history in the Middle West has
done the least about it.

—GEORGE STARK, PRESIDENT OF THE
DETROIT HISTORICAL SOCIETY

GEORGE Stark's comment closely resembles Clarence Burton's observation from a dozen years earlier. Whereas Burton suggested that Detroit
was the largest U.S. city without a historical museum, Stark reflected
that the progress made since was woefully inadequate. After joining the board
in 1941, he assumed the reins of the Society in 1942 and immediately set about
addressing this problem.

Stark was a larger-than-life, old-fashioned newspaperman. Not the angry,
gruff, loud type but the gentlemanly, well-spoken, make-things-happen-with-a-
smile type. At least that was his public image. As a columnist and editor at
the *Detroit News*, he wielded significant political weight but was seldom heavy-
handed. The subtlety of his statement above is typical and arguably more critical of City leaders than of the Society. It was those community leaders whom
he enlisted to address the problems.

Early in his tenure, he embarked on two museum tours: one along the East

Coast and the second in middle America. In Krum's words, he "returned brimfull of the concern over the backwardness of support for the Detroit Historical Museum. From his [newspaper] column, like an electric spark, spread an impulse to better this condition."

At his first Annual Meeting, a luncheon affair on January 16, 1943, in the English Room at the Statler Hotel, Stark rolled out the big guns. Mayor Edward Jeffries Jr. was the guest of honor. Monsignor Edward Hickey, a long-time DHS trustee and chancellor of the Diocese of Detroit, gave the invocation. Harvey Campbell, of the Detroit Board of Commerce, was the guest speaker. And for pizzazz, Detroit automotive pioneer Charles B. King, the first man to design, build, and drive a gasoline-powered car on Detroit streets and one of Stark's many friends, came in from New York.

In early February, Stark sent a long and detailed letter to the Board of Commissioners of the Detroit Institute of Arts, which had recently granted $1,500 per annum. He outlined a budget of $9,000 that included double the allotment for museum rent, reasonable salaries for three staff positions—director, curator, and clerical—and money to move the collection to an appropriate space. There was even a 5 percent contingency written in. This was at least three times any earlier budget outline. He suggested that the City, through the DIA commissioners, should donate $4,000.

Stark admitted that this was aggressive but stated, "There are indications of a revived interest in the aims of the Detroit Historical Society," suggesting marked revenue growth. He described again the poor state of the current facility and activities of trustees to identify better locations. "You will agree this is a tremendously vital program, and one that has been sadly neglected here."

A significant break came in May. Stark had taken his crusade on the luncheon circuit and at one event caught the ear of Mary (Mrs. Fred T.) Murphy. Mary was the sister-in-law of Francis (Mrs. Charles B.) Pike of Chicago, the last surviving daughter of General Russell A. Alger, who was a Civil War commander, Michigan governor, U.S. secretary of war, and Michigan lumber and railroad magnate. In 1900, there were few Detroiters more revered than Alger, and despite a fountain in Grand Circus Park, his daughter was looking for a more lasting memorial.

Murphy, Stark, and future DHS trustee and museum architect William Kapp, a director at Smith, Hinchman and Grylls, went to Chicago to meet with Mrs. Pike. She proposed a donation of $50,000 to the Society's building effort, assuming that the Society would raise $200,000 to build a suitable structure in which to house a hall dedicated to her father. In Krum's words, "There could be but one answer from Detroit leaders, and the Society went to work."

The first step was reimagining the Society's staff structure and establishing several significant new partnerships. Following months of behind-the-scenes work, trustees met on June 10, 1943, and were introduced to their new director. Robert Larson, a trustee of the Michigan Historical Society, would be in charge of both the Society and the museum. Miss Butler remained in the curator position. Julia Hubbard, now DHS secretary, remained leader of the Junior Group, but after brief remarks from her the trustees voted not to extend honorary memberships to the youths. This program faded but has been revived in various forms numerous times since.

Stark enthusiastically announced at the same meeting that the Common Council had approved the Arts Commission's recommendation and increased its annual appropriation to $6,500—a significant win for the president. Additionally, arrangements were made with the Board of Education to store the Society's artifacts when an eventual move took place. In the meantime, operations at Barlum Tower continued with the addition of a small suite of offices. Furniture for this space was donated by the J. L. Hudson Company. The new administration was welcomed to their "official headquarters" at a reception hosted by Hazel (Mrs. Wilson W.) Mills on June 16.

Mrs. Mills, daughter of revered former Detroit Mayor Hazen Pingree, represented another aspect of Stark's style: putting the Board of Trustees to work and further engaging the business community. Mills's appointment as chairman of the Membership Committee in 1945 energized that group and resulted in fantastic growth over the next few years. The membership doubled in five years to 2,282, and two years later topped 3,300—reportedly the largest for a local history organization in North America. Memberships of different types were developed, notably the Business Founders group—an offshoot of the Business Pioneers relationship.

In November 1943, the Building Endowment Fund Committee was launched under the direction of Dr. Frank Cody, superintendent of Detroit Public Schools. Also tasked with leadership were Dr. David Henry, executive president of Wayne University, McPherson Browning of the Detroit Trust Company, and Harold Hastings, secretary-manager of the Adcraft Club of Detroit. Leonard Simons of the Simons-Michelson Advertising Co. (later Simons-Michelson-Zieve) offered the firm's services pro bono to promote the museum building project. His offer was accepted, and he was elected to the leadership group. Simons became a driving creative force at the DHS and a significant ally for many of Stark's initiatives.

Not long afterward, a roster of 32 men and women was announced for the general Building Fund Committee. It included some notable names including Briggs, Larned, Lodge, Murphy, Shapiro, Vernor, and Wilson. Mayor Edward Jeffries accepted the honorary chairmanship. At the Twenty-Second Annual Meeting in January 1944, the committee reported that in two short months, $130,000 (about $2 million today) had been raised toward the overall goal. With enthusiasm running high, a fundraising consultant was hired and given a promotional budget of $9,000 and donated office space in the Penobscot Building. In October, the trustees approved hiring a full-time publicist also, and at Stark's recommendation Mrs. May McKaig got the job.

Prospects were improving for the acquisition of a temporary home on the expanding campus of Wayne University. At this juncture, the university was still part of the Detroit Board of Education. With Cody, Henry, and Dr. Raymond Miller, head of the History Department, on the DHS Board of Trustees, the relationship was poised for success. In order to facilitate funding for the temporary facility, it was "deemed desirable by both parties hereto to provide for a closer association between the University and the Society." The university budget was made the vehicle for City of Detroit support, which increased to $10,000 for that fiscal year. In a formal agreement drafted in July 1944, the university promised to provide an adequate building for the museum and to accept stewardship of the Society's artifacts during this transition period, with the stated intent that the Society be responsible for handling and maintaining the collection.

Momentum was building and great strides were realized in 1945. January marked the inaugural issue of the *Detroit Historical Society Bulletin*. Though not the Society's first attempt at publishing, it was the most successful, lasting twenty-five years. It fell under the aegis of Director Robert Larson and was funded by a grant from the Wayne County Board of Supervisors for the first few years. Like any good membership magazine, the *Bulletin* consistently delivered a variety of Society information monthly, generally with a hiatus during the summer.

Within its pages—initially eight, but later up to twenty-four—readers could find regular correspondence from the various directors, presidents, and later the Detroit Historical Commission expressing the hopes and dreams for the

This home at 441 Merrick Street, on the Wayne University campus, became the second home to the Detroit Historical Society's museum between 1945 and 1951.

In 1949, J. Bell Moran, Miss Gracie Krum, and Mrs. Arthur Hampton look at a photograph of Arthur Hampton, the museum's first curator from 1928 to 1942.

organization's future. Each issue contained staff and trustee profiles, event calendars, reviews of exhibitions, programs, donations to the collection, and at least one or two historical articles about events or people in Detroit's past.

Perhaps most importantly for this current text, the *Bulletin* picks up the Society's story about the time that Gracie Krum's valuable narrative wraps up in 1951. There is a wonderful overlap, with the house organ becoming the ever-more-confident public face of the Society, and Krum providing the commentary of one who has been there from the beginning. Despite her staid, professional style, it is clear that she is excited by the groundswell of interest for the mission that Society founders had envisioned.

In the spirit of youth programming and education, the Society sponsored an Essay and Oratorical Contest that was held in schools across the city. The final presentations took place at Rackham Auditorium on the evening of April 20, 1945, with six students receiving war bonds for their efforts.

Wayne University identified a building to become the new Detroit Historical Museum, and the home itself was soon historic. Located at 441 Merrick Street, just west of Cass Avenue, this rambling Arts and Crafts cottage had been the boyhood home of G. Mennen Williams, who would become governor of Michigan in 1949. In phases, the university was purchasing a significant number of tracts in what had been a very upscale residential neighborhood. Many of the homes were repurposed as classroom space, offices, or laboratories, so a historical archive and exhibitions galleries fit well into this amalgam. Over time, most residences were removed and replaced by modern campus facilities. Fortunately, a number of homes remain on Wayne State University's urban campus today as a reminder of its rich (literally) history.

The location of the Williams House was nearly ideal. It was a few hundred yards from the main branch of the Detroit Public Library and the Burton Historical Collection, and a few hundred yards more from the Detroit Institute of Arts, where many Society artifacts were in basement storage. What it *wasn't* was a hundred yards in the air, needing elevator access. On a classically beautiful, tree-lined street in the heart of the city's growing Cultural District, this made a nice temporary location.

### UPDATING THE EQUATION

On May 7, 1945, President George Stark presented the trustees with an idea that would guide public history initiatives in Detroit for over six decades. In discussions with City Councilman John Lodge, the concept of a municipal Historical Commission emerged that would prioritize the City's investment in important material culture. The Society's position was described as similar to that of "the Founders Society to the Art Institute," indicating control of the buildings, exhibits, and collection would fall to the commission, and in turn to a Detroit Historical Department, with the Society directing ancillary needs in the form of program direction, membership support, and funding. To do this would take a voter-approved amendment to the City Charter.

At this same meeting, it was announced that Wayne University was "loaning" the Society its Department of History chairman, DHS trustee Raymond Miller, to become director of the Society for one year. Robert Larson was named "Assistant to the Director." Miss Krum notes that Miller effected a general shakeup, and "the entire personnel of the Museum staff was changed." Indeed, only a few months later Larson "severed connections" with the organization. Not long afterward he was replaced by Henry D. Brown, who had a master's degree in history from the University of Michigan and spent five years curating the university's Michigan Historical Collection (now housed at the Bentley Historical Library). When Miller returned to leading Wayne's History Department in 1947, Brown was named as the new director of the Society and museums. Much as Stark's association with the Society had changed its trajectory, so would Brown leave a lasting legacy.

The immediate priorities for Miller in 1945 were two: moving the museum and offices to Merrick Street and organizing the archival material at the DIA, presumably in anticipation of it finding a new home. On the Charter Amendment side, the "Ad Guys" took over. There were frequent meetings at the Adcraft Club for trustees Harold Hastings, Leonard Simons, and Reuben Ryding, all marketing and public relations executives in a hugely competitive market.

With the foundation well laid, Stark presented a formal resolution to the trustees in mid-August. In it he proposed that, since "maintenance of such an historical museum is widely accepted as a public function," the City of Detroit should form the historical commission. The Society would relinquish its 15,000 artifacts and the $250,000 in the building fund, as long as the City agreed to "use the money herein proffered, and such other money as may be available, to build and equip an historical museum." The museum director was tasked with providing—in a loosely worded directive—such rooms for the Society as, "in its opinion, are reasonably adequate for the headquarters of the Detroit Historical Society and shall permit occupancy of such rooms without charge or rent." The Ad Guys did their job and celebrated the passage of the Charter Amendment in the "Club Room" of their new home on Merrick Street.

It was a celebratory crowd that gathered for the 1946 Annual Meeting at the Wardell-Sheraton Hotel (later the Park Sheraton, then Park Shelton). Miller was the speaker. Brown was the toastmaster. Stark's presidential report was his last, enumerating successful attainment of the three main goals: get out of Barlum Tower, raise a quarter million dollars for a museum, and have the City assume management of the physical assets. Following his remarks, City Clerk Thomas Leadbetter swore in the new Detroit Historical Commission consisting of Stark, who became its president, Leonard Simons, Mary Murphy, and Donald Kiskadden—all Society trustees—with rolling four-year terms that eventually lasted until 1966, lending a needed stability. Two weeks later, the DHS trustees met and elected Dr. Alfred Whittaker president.

Expansion of the Board of Trustees through this period is also impressive. In 1945, it consisted of five officers and nine trustees, nine men and five women. Two years later, the board had expanded to twenty-four trustees, six of them women. More notable was the growth of board participation. Only a few committees had existed in 1945, primarily membership, lectures, and women's. By 1947 it had exploded to twenty, including those addressing programs and public relations, liaison with the City, and various curatorial topics like Native Americans, medicine, and maritime. The Society's affairs were increasingly carried on through committee work, the board acting as a general clearinghouse and administrative center.

In just thirty-six months, Krum described the Society as a changed organization, and these rapid changes came at a perfect time. George Stark and his compatriots had gotten Detroit fired up about its history in physical and monetary terms. The Great Depression had scarred Detroit deeply, and after struggling through World War II, residents were hungry for projects that reflected upbeat narratives highlighting America's broad, but not universal, perception of greatness. Patriotic fervor—specifically how the Yankees beat the French and Brits and Indians (and Southerners in some homes)—remained a large part of the postwar landscape, and the Historical Commission's brick-and-mortar projects caught the imagination of history fans in the community and naturally the project ballooned.

There soon emerged a contingent promoting the Museum of Great Lakes History in a schooner on Belle Isle, led by trustee Prentiss Brown, and another contingent advocating for preservation efforts at Fort Wayne and its historic buildings. Both were important projects. The first would preserve the last active sailing vessel on the Great Lakes. The second involved a site that represents centuries of recorded history, starting with significant Native American habitation, pre–Civil War fortifications, and a possible Underground Railroad crossing point.

The schooner *J. T. Wing* was donated to the City by Grant Piggott of the J. T. Wing Company, Joseph Braun of Braun Lumber, and investor Oscar Johnson. No longer profitable as a working ship, it underwent a yearlong refit in a slip near the Ambassador Bridge, and then a triumphal voyage to its final berth on

The retired schooner *J. T. Wing* housed the Museum of Great Lakes History on Belle Isle from 1949 to 1956.

Belle Isle on July 24, 1948. Opened the following year, the vessel was under the supervision of Captain Joseph E. Johnson, who formed a crew of volunteer tour guides and founded the Great Lakes Model Shipbuilders Guild, which, in turn, launched *Telescope* magazine in 1952. This publication, specifically addressing Great Lakes maritime history, is still being produced today.

Besides the modelers' guild, which became the Great Lakes Maritime Institute (GLMI) in 1960, the *J. T. Wing* also received extensive assistance from members of the Marine Historical Society of Detroit (MHSD), which had been founded in 1944. In the fourth edition of the new *Bulletin*, the MHSD supplied the introduction and expressed hope that someday it could have an archive and meeting room in the new museum once it was built. While that did not happen, it continued to support the Society's efforts to advance Detroit maritime history. Its publication, the *Detroit Marine Historian*, is now in its seventy-third volume.

On June 14, 1950, the military museum at Fort Wayne was officially opened. The U.S. Army maintained parts of the campus for induction and administrative

The barracks building, built between 1839 and 1842, became the centerpiece of the Fort Wayne Military Museum (later Historic Fort Wayne) and regularly hosted encampments and reenactments (c. 1989).

purposes into the 1970s, and the Army Corps of Engineers continues to maintain a survey facility there as of this writing. However, the old star fort was designated as surplus and given to the City of Detroit. It thus fell under the Historical Commission's purview, adding yet another thematic facility to the City's historic holdings, ripe for development.

Despite these great strides, the best was yet to come.

### A VISION REALIZED

In 1950, J. Bell Moran was again elected president of the Society. Following the war, he had resumed active involvement and along with Stark, Simons, Miller, and Brown was focused on realizing their ultimate goal: building a proper Detroit Historical Museum. It did not come easily.

In his monthly entries in the Society's *Bulletin*, bylined "From the Big Desk," Dr. Miller outlined efforts to obtain a site in the Cultural Center. The ideal property, suggested by Burton in 1930, was north of the library on West Kirby Street, with frontage on Woodward Avenue. Indeed, seventeen years later, with that site settled on, it seemed that the plans were in flux from month to month. In June 1947, Miller wrote that "after wandering around on paper, the museum is nailed down," with the first unit occupying the west half of the frontage between Woodward and Cass, with entrance on Kirby. It was suggested that a second phase would complete the Kirby facade to Woodward.

By January 1948, the two phases were swapped, William Kapp was developing the drawings, and according to commission president Stark, "plans for the building will proceed now at full speed." The City Plan Commission released a graphic indicating that the Society's footprint not only occupied the entire block of Kirby but also extended north along Woodward to Ferry Street—prime real estate that was never acquired for the museum.

During this due diligence phase, the major players studied many museums, primarily east of the Mississippi. Miller and then Brown made two-week reconnaissance tours in the East, much as Stark had done a few years earlier. Several of the trustees offered similar input based on their travels in North America and Europe. Kapp was more involved than most, also visiting numerous other museums and creating several renderings for various sites, all without remuneration. It wasn't until the final drawings were being prepared that Kapp and his firm signed a formal contract for services to be rendered.

By May of the following year, Kapp's drawings were published in the *Bulletin*. He, Stark, and Brown appear on the cover of the magazine with a distinctive white-on-white architectural model. The proposed building had elements of classicism to blend with neighboring structures but bore essentially the midcentury modern design that the building represents today. Sketches show that initially the central rotunda feature was far more prominent and the Kirby entrance more imposing.

At this time, the building fund had grown to $400,000 and included a sizable gift—$135,000, the largest to date—from the families of John and Horace Dodge for a hall dedicated to Detroit industry. The Historical Commission scheduled the groundbreaking for July 24, the day that Monsieur Cadillac established a French outpost on the shores of the Detroit River and long celebrated as the city's birthday. The *J. T. Wing* had already started this tradition the year prior for its trip to Belle Isle, and the Society would continue to dedicate buildings, open exhibitions, and schedule programs on July 24 for years to come.

Indeed, it was understood by all concerned that the new Detroit Historical Museum would open in 1951 on the 250th anniversary of Cadillac's landing. Two years was a tight time frame, and perhaps it was this pressure, and a

George Stark, William Kapp, and Henry Brown (left to right) review model of proposed Detroit Historical Museum in spring 1949.

George Stark, William Kapp, Mary Murphy, Leonard Simons, Donald Kiskadden, and Henry Brown (left to right) at groundbreaking for Detroit Historical Museum, July 24, 1949.

Concrete footings and wall forms are in place for initial foundation of Detroit Historical Museum in 1950.

tangible end in sight, that made the sod-turning ceremony fun. The small crowd was smiling—guarded smiles perhaps—but there was relief in this significant step. There was no turning back now.

The first phase was projected to be a quarter of the planned build-out, including Dodge Hall, the large gallery closest to Woodward, the rotunda and main entrance facing Woodward, as well as the gallery spaces along Kirby that today are Stark and Alger halls, and the stairways that are now part of the Kirby entrance. In all, the building was four stories tall, with open space on the lower level and third floor for additional smaller installations. Society offices were located in the old carriage house at the rear of the property, which had formerly been a creative arts school called Children's House.

Following the groundbreaking, progress must have seemed painfully slow. After thirteen months, there was only a hole in the ground with basic foundational footings. Under the direction of general contracting firm O. W. Burke & Co., and with less than a year to go, work progressed quickly. By October, the concrete beams that support the main floor were in place over the lower level, and by November the steel upper structure was nearly completed.

Off-site, designers and museum preparators were developing the materials that would gradually fill the museum with exhibitions that "illustrate the development of the American Way of Life and standard of living here in our own Detroit." In buildings at Fort Wayne, preparators Richard Jennings, Jack Burton, and Frank Caito were busy fabricating signs and display cases for the new museum. The opening program cites numerous businesses and organizations that helped finance and, in some cases, create the individual exhibitions.

Dedication of the museum was part of a grand, three-day spectacle focused on Detroit's 250th birthday. Commencing at 5 p.m. on July 24, 1951, the dais in front of the museum featured ambassadors from France, Great Britain, and Canada, native sons Governor G. Mennen (Soapy) Williams, Ralph Bunche, a director at the United Nations, and Mayor Albert Cobo, as well as numerous local dignitaries. The full birthday celebration included a re-creation of Cadillac's landing with costumed interpreters in canoes, band concerts on Belle Isle and Campus Martius, banquets, memorials, a river parade of a thousand pleasure boats, and fireworks in both Windsor and Detroit.

Among the first interior spaces dedicated was the Russell A. Alger Memorial Hall of Patriotism on the second floor (then referenced as the mezzanine), fulfilling the commitment to Mrs. Pike's icebreaking donation. Adjoining that was the Rooms of Tradition sponsored by the Historic Memorials Association. Along the north side of the building was the John and Horace Dodge Memorial Hall of Industry, a towering gallery that could accommodate both exhibitions and pageants.

In time, Round Hall would hold a number of intricate dioramas underwritten by the J. L. Hudson Company and created by Bartlett Frost. The "Streets of Old Detroit" on the lower level was a gradual process—the 1870s section came in 1951, the 1840s opened on July 24, 1954, and the 1900s was built in conjunction with the Kresge wing in 1966. The "Wolverine Model Railroad Club" layout, the "Old Newsboys/Goodfellows," and "Metropolitan Services" would fill out the third-floor spaces, along with a Gallery of Citizenship that featured the rotating "Teacher of the Month" and "Historic Citizen of the Month" displays.

## NEW FACES, NEW VOICES

While the building project was in process, other major pieces were being put in place. These included expansion of the Historical Department's staff, the exhi-

The 1870s portion of the "Streets of Old Detroit" was the first to be installed in 1951. Museum staff salvaged portions of actual buildings being cleared during the city's urban renewal to bring authenticity to the installation.

Detroit Historical Museum staff posed for a photograph soon after the museum opened in 1951.

bitions and programs, and the degree of public involvement with the Society, which generally promoted membership and fundraising.

Growth of the Historical Department staff included some personalities that would influence the museums for many years. Bartlett Frost was hired as assistant director of museums in 1948, a year after Henry Brown's promotion to director. Frost had an extensive museum résumé, having worked in Illinois and Colorado and for the National Park Service in California. He was a renowned diorama artist but in Detroit would be most associated with his work on the "Streets of Old Detroit."

Margot Pearsall joined the staff soon after Frost and was put in charge of the Department of Social History and was the supervisor of records—the first curator and collections manager under the new regime. She came to the museum from the Midwest Museums Conference, after service in France with the Red Cross. Pearsall's first assignment was the period installations in the Rooms of Tradition gallery, and she assisted on the "Streets of Old Detroit" and the Hall of Patriotism. She was later named senior curator and was recognized with the Top 10 Working Women of Detroit award in 1968.

Glenn Stille (Stil-ee), having studied anthropology at the University of Kentucky, joined the staff in July 1951. After a stint in the U.S. Army, he returned as curator of the Fort Wayne Military Museum and was instrumental in early fort preservation and interpretation. Also notable among the preparatory staff was Robert Wright, the first African American professional hired by the department, and Robert Lee, who would become the first curator of the Dossin Great Lakes Museum.

Museum lectures over the previous two decades had always featured regional historians and subject matter experts. Such presentations continued as regular curator chats for many years. The program added a formal element in June 1948, when the first of the annual Lewis Cass Lectures was presented at the Book-Cadillac Hotel. Hallmarks of the Cass lectures were two: they fea-

A 1900-era parlor is depicted in this portion of the "Period Rooms" gallery located on the Detroit Historical Museum's top floor in 1954.

tured nationally recognized scholars speaking on regional topics; and their lectures were published for distribution to Society members and local libraries. Along with scholarly articles in the *Bulletin*, the lectures fulfilled a significant portion of the Society's mission.

Increased profile was partly due to increased cooperation. The Society was a founding partner in the conference known as "Michigan in Perspective: Local History Conference." Spearheaded by Wayne State University Professor Philip Mason in 1958, it involved numerous regional historical organizations including the Michigan Historical Society and the Algonquin Club of Detroit and Windsor. Now produced by the Historical Society of Michigan, attendance at its sixty-second event in 2019 drew over seven hundred people.

The American Association of State and Local History has also been a long-time partner. Henry Brown served on the council for many years and as president from 1964 to 1966. The Society hosted the AASLH annual conference in 1953 and 2014—also held in Dearborn in 1991, but no record suggests Society's sponsorship—and has been recognized numerous times with Awards of Merit. It also received the prestigious History in Progress award in 2018. Brown was elected president of the Michigan Historical Society in September 1957. The DHS has also been a long-time member of the American Association of Museums (today the American Alliance of Museums), hosting its conference in 1961, and the Mid-West Museums Conference (today the Association of Midwest Museums).

Outreach efforts were many. In late 1947, under the direction of Reuben Ryding, chairman of the Public Information Committee, the Society began to get regular airtime on local radio stations. Partnering with Wayne University's Radio Guild, "The Streets of Detroit" was aired every Wednesday evening on WWJ, discussing the history behind city street names. On Monday and Friday evenings, "Our Town—Detroit in History" reached audiences on WJLB with features about everything from historical characters to Christmas in Detroit. By January 1948, WJR was working with the Society on "Know Your America," and WXYZ's *George and Anne* show featured stories of old Detroit. The following year, the Society's Business Founders group was underwriting an audio-visual filmstrip project with Detroit Public Schools and Wayne University to get Detroit history into public and parochial schools. Along with the regular publicity received in Stark's "Town Talk" column in the *Detroit News*, and a growing number of television appearances, the Society's media presence was significantly increased.

Besides professional programming, regular membership events took on a more festive atmosphere. The Annual Meetings became staged galas that included live music and a historically themed fashion show, often drawing over

The "Collector's Corner" exhibit featured rotating installations of items that Detroiters collected. From dolls and housewares, as seen here in 1963, to paintings and firearms.

An exhibit preparator works in the fabrication laboratory located at Fort Wayne Military Museum in 1953.

four hundred people. In 1952, the museum and the Detroit Historical Society Guild hosted the first Patriot's Ball, a gathering of over thirty patriotic organizations in the Detroit area that included a colorful Parade of Flags and costumed flag-bearers, as well as speeches, a program, and entertainment by the Vaughn Monroe Orchestra.

The annual Indian-Pilgrim Dinner was also a patriotic affair that emphasized multiculturalism, aboriginal heritage, and "authentic" early American cuisine. The Christmas Open House was, for many years, a pageant featuring choirs, invocations, and Christmas trees, with holiday decorations throughout the "Streets of Old Detroit" courtesy of the DHS Guild. Similarly focused was a short-lived Sunday Parlor Organ series featuring the singing of favorite Christian hymns in the Period Alcoves gallery. The annual, two-week-long Children's Book Fair brought in hundreds of families; by 1956 over fifty thousand people were accommodated over several weeks at author talks on bleachers in Dodge Hall. Old-Timers Day on Belle Isle, with its vintage baseball game, was also an annual affair.

Indeed, entering the tenth year of the partnership with the City, things were humming along nicely. The three facilities were hosting almost three hundred thousand people annually, and the Woodward museum had surpassed one million visitors. The Historical Department boasted a staff of over forty-five, who along with volunteers and Guild members facilitated seventy-three exhibits and events in 1954.

It was arguably a golden period for experiencing Detroit history. Significant donations had enriched the collection, including items from the inventors Charles Brady King, Henry Leland, William Stout, and Thomas C. Clark. Additionally, several books about Detroit were published in this period, including those by Society leaders Stark, Miller, Frank B. Woodford, and Milo Quaife. The volume *Detroit in Its World Setting* (first edition) was edited by Rae Elizabeth Rips, DPL History and Travel Department chief, and Great Lakes–themed pieces came out by Harlan Hatcher and Walter Havigurst. Newspaperman Malcolm Bingay's often irreverent *Detroit Is My Own Home Town* was balanced by Frederick Lieb's book about the Detroit Tigers baseball team and Rev. George Paré's history of the Roman Catholic Church in Detroit. F. Clever Bald penned *Detroit's First American Decade*. Perhaps most notable was Dr. Alice Crathern's study of the contributions of women to the City titled *In Detroit . . . Courage Was the Fashion*. These, along with published Cass lectures, gave curious Detroiters plenty to absorb.

It was also during this period that exhibition design was making a slow transition from largely object-based installations to those more attuned to people and organizations. Early displays, both at Barlum Tower and Merrick Street, included titles like "Lighting of Yesteryear," "Medical Practice in Detroit as Shown by Instruments and Medications, 1847–1947," "Arts and Crafts of the Gentlewoman," and "Inflation over the Years." The new museum featured happy titles like the fundraising display "Bonnets That Bloom in the Spring" but also community-focused offerings like "A Century of Negro Life and Culture" (1952), "Women of Achievement" (1953), and "Jewish Life and Culture in Detroit" (1954). It should be noted that in 1956 curatorial staff mounted an artifact-rich exhibit, based on recently acquired Native American material from the collection of former trustee Carl Clark. While culturally diverse, its title—*"INDIANS!!!"*—was more apropos of a John Wayne movie than an enlightened exhibition but certainly a reflection of the times.

Object-based displays were not gone. The first "Curator's Corner" appeared in March 1954, rotating material from individual collectors on a short-term basis. There were also numerous one- to three-month exhibits touching on everything from firefighting equipment to sheet music. Patriotism remained a theme, with "Freedom Shrine" and "Old Glory" shows featured during this period. The Guild's commitment to historic fashion grew stronger with time.

It would be appropriate to remember several supporters who would not see the next phases of museum building but who had worked valiantly to lay the foundation. Trustee Agnes Burton, who had assumed the secretary position from Gracie Krum and Mabel Smith, died in 1948. Carl L. Clark, a student and collector of Native American culture, spearheaded the Indian-Pilgrim Dinner until his death in 1953. An endowment in his name had grown to over $92,000 by 1966. Mary Murphy, conduit to the Alger funds that seeded the museum building program, passed away in 1956. Krum, a visionary, teacher, and champion of Detroit's recorded history, died in August 1957.

## ONWARD AND UPWARD

Stark first posed the possibility of moving into Phase 2 of the Kirby building project in early 1955, citing the need for more room. Within a year, the Society received news that caused it to put that project on hold and pivot to a more critical need. Soon after the *J. T. Wing* opened for the season on April 2, City building inspectors began assessing the extent to which dry rot had affected the aging wooden hull. She was rotting when first landed at Belle Isle, and some critics at the time questioned the wisdom of investing in the ship at all.

Curator Bob Lee later recounted that toward the end of the year an inspector returned and essentially pushed his finger deep into the base of one of the masts. The inspector told Captain Joseph Johnson that the ship was no longer safe for visitors. The Society announced the closing of the Museum of Great Lakes History in early October, with its last day to be October 30, 1956.

Over the winter, the artifacts, models, display cases, and any running rigging worth salvaging were removed to storage or a temporary exhibition set up in the lower level of the Detroit Historical Museum. As the vessel itself was too fragile to move, the decision was made to burn her where she sat. Fire Chief Ed Blohm turned the project over to the local Civil Defense battalion as a practice site. The biggest logistical problem was getting waterlogged beams a foot thick to ignite.

According to *Detroit Free Press* columnist Mark Beltaire, the *Wing* was loaded with "1,000 gallons of fuel oil, 1,000 gallons of drain oil, four 10-yard loads of cleaner sludge, and 150 old tires"—not a method that would be condoned today. Cans of gasoline were strategically placed, all hatches were opened for ventilation, and the crowd kept at a good distance. At 12:30 p.m. on Saturday, November 3, 1956, Inspector Harry Reeves, a respected marksman, used a machine gun with tracer rounds to ignite the gasoline, and the conflagration grew from there. The fireboat *James Kendall*, as well as the museum's other vessel, the Huron boat *Helen McLeod*, stood by as sentinels. Freighters passing on the river offered whistle salutes. It was a grand exit for the *J. T. Wing*.

It was also a great way for the people of Detroit to find out that they needed a new maritime museum. One family received that message loud and clear, facilitated by Leonard Simons. Less than six weeks after the *J. T. Wing* stopped smoldering, the Dossin family stepped forward with a donation of $125,000, to be matched by the City, for construction of a new museum building. Dossin Food Products bottled and distributed Pepsi-Cola and Nehi products, among others. They were also avid boaters and boat racers, owning a series of hydroplanes sporting variations on the name *Miss Pepsi*.

Originally styled the Dossin Marine Museum, it eventually opened as the Dossin Great Lakes Museum—a nod to its place as the first building constructed specifically to tell the freshwater maritime story. However, work needed to be done before that was accomplished. The Belle Isle location was to remain the same; the area around the ashes of the *J. T. Wing* was filled and bulldozed to accommodate a terrestrial structure. A portion of the *Wing*'s lagoon was preserved and remains today.

Again, Bill Kapp sharpened his pencil and created a structure that the City could afford. From a structural standpoint, a museum is a curious thing to put in such a beautiful location. In the years before ultraviolet window filters and LED lights, museums had few windows: sunlight deteriorates artifacts and challenges environmental controls like heating and cooling. Kapp had to minimize light from the natural southern exposure of the lot. His solution was a long rectangle on a north-south orientation with small windows in the clerical areas, two isolated viewing areas (an upper and lower level) looking toward the river and Canada, and only one window in the gallery spaces facing west (which was soon covered over).

Small by today's standards, its gallery space was substantial, if linear—about 4,000 square feet, with an additional 900-square-foot gallery set near the river. Plans were included for a riverfront auditorium to the west that would come when funding allowed. Behind-the-scenes space included an office, a library, storage, an employee locker room, and an exhibit prep and modeler's workshop. A two-bedroom apartment was included upstairs for the onsite curator. A photography lab and darkroom were shoehorned under the stairs.

Site development began on May 21, 1959, when Councilwoman Mary Beck, Robert Dossin, and George Stark broke ground. The target date: July 24, 1960. The general contractor was Salvaggio and Sons, and by early February, the exterior structure was nearing completion. When July rolled around, much of the material, models, flags, and displays that had come off the *J. T. Wing* were ensconced in their new home. Later in the year, the periscope of the USS *Tambor*, a submarine until recently stationed at the Brodhead Naval Armory half a mile away, was installed through the roof, where it remains today. Captain Johnson had retired, so DHM preparator Bob Lee, a transportation specialist, was appointed curator of the Dossin Great Lakes Museum.

The dedication ceremony was officiated by Admiral Leon J. Jacobi, U.S. Navy (Retired), with an invocation by Rev. Father Edward Dowling, S.J., blessing of the building by Rev. Elmer Usher of Mariners Church, and a benediction by Rabbi Milton Rosenbaum. Mayor Louis Miriani, Councilman Eugene Van Antwerp, and George Stark made comments, Donald Dossin unveiled a donors plaque, and Mary (Mrs. Roy L.) Dossin christened the building with a bottle containing water from the five Great Lakes. The audience was packed with other Dossin family members, Society trustees, City of Detroit dignitaries, and numerous maritime history fans.

Appropriately, three years later, a pavilion was constructed adjacent to the museum's main entrance to display permanently the Dossin family's most successful *Miss Pepsi* hydroplane. Soon afterward, with help from the Great Lakes Maritime Institute, Marine Historical Society of Detroit, DHS Guild, and thousands of schoolchildren's pennies, the museum was able to purchase and install the elegant Gothic Room from the palatial steamer *City of Detroit III*. It took almost two years to clean the white oak of the former men's smoking lounge to create a stunning entrance feature for the museum.

The final piece of the original puzzle fell into place a few years later thanks to a donation from Helen DeRoy, widow of auto executive and boat racing fan Aaron DeRoy. According to Curator Lee, his staff was working on the Gothic Room when

At the 1959 groundbreaking, Councilwoman Mary Beck, Robert Dossin, and George Stark show Pamela Knighton and Doug and Sidonie Dossin a model of the new museum.

Admiral Leon Jacobi (USNR) leads the dedication ceremony at the Dossin Great Lakes Museum in 1960.

Family and friends gather to watch *Miss Pepsi* installed in her special pavilion at the museum in 1963.

the niece of Mrs. DeRoy, who lived across from Belle Isle in the Whittier Tower, came into the museum, got a quick tour, and asked, "What do you need?" Lee replied, "An auditorium." Kapp had included it in his original plans—in today's terms, a shovel-ready project—and Mrs. DeRoy soon visited the museum and agreed to fund Aaron DeRoy Hall. It was dedicated in April 1968.

There were still neat projects ahead for the Belle Isle museum, but important things also were happening on Woodward.

## THE NEXT STEP

In everyone's mind—those who had been through the initial Detroit Historical Museum design phase—there was no doubt that the museum would eventually extend from Woodward to Cass Avenues along Kirby, much as the Rackham Memorial Building does on Farnsworth Street between Woodward and John R. In theory, the two would create a nice symmetry within the city's Cultural Center. Designed to be built in phases, the fund for Phase 2 grew slowly; by 1961 it was $38,640 thanks to $25,000 from Helen Louise Tuller Miller's estate. An opportunity to build the second phase came on July 15, 1964, when Sebastian Kresge, retail pioneer and president of the Kresge Foundation, donated $500,000 to the City for the next wing of the museum. Former Society president and long-time trustee Gordon Rice is credited with initiating the conversation with Mr. Kresge, and the commissioners convinced Mayor Jerome Cavanagh to include the matching funds in his budget.

This was all good news, as there had been a number of lean years. The first inklings of financial shortfalls appear in the mid-1950s. Stark stated it clearly in the January 1958 *Bulletin*: "This is no time for reckless spending; in fact, it is no time for spending at all, except where dire necessity dictates." Notably the newsletter shrank from twenty-four to sixteen pages immediately, and only twelve pages in 1960, the first year that the annual report does not occupy the pre-meeting issue of the *Bulletin* in January. Judging from a December column by Stark, the Christmas Open House was saved from cancellation only by some of Santa's generous "helpers."

In November 1960, Brown notes a reduction in City funding due to population decline. Whereas museum hours during the summer had customarily been 1 p.m. to 10 p.m., they were changed from 9 a.m. to 6 p.m. Staff recently hired for the Dossin meant the reduction of one position each at the DHM and Fort Wayne. This came as overall attendance was topping half a million annually and expected to rise.

Brown visited Antoine Cadillac–related sites in France in 1962 with two of George Pierrot's film associates. Pierrot was a seasoned traveler and hosted a popular travelogue feature called "The World Adventure Series." It started with a live audience on Sunday afternoons at the Detroit Institute of Arts auditorium and was later broadcast on television several days a week in the 1960s. The result of this partnership was a film called *Cadillac's Homeland*, which earned Brown and the filmmakers another AASLH award. That same year, the Society Guild produced a film, in partnership with industrial film company Jam Handy Organization, titled *Journey to Yesterday*. It was used as a vehicle to promote the museums and prepare school groups for a visit.

These two video releases were feathers in the Society's cap, but there were also two notable losses during this time. Donald Kiskadden, a long-time trustee and a founding member of the Detroit Historical Commission, died in July 1963. A similar Society stalwart was Thomas Starr, a Lincolniana collector who became part of Dossin museum lore when he commandeered a park full of benches for a USS *Dubuque* charity cruise one year and got arrested for that action as he returned them. A member since 1929 and a trustee since 1933, his powerful personality passed in 1965.

Nineteen sixty-six was a year of tremendous ups and downs. On January 10, the Historical Commission celebrated two decades of accomplishments in

This photograph of the Detroit Historical Society trustees was taken in the Detroit Historical Museum's Gallery of Citizenship in 1954. Captured here are, from the left: Harold Hastings, Henry Brown, Ben Marsh, Julia Hubbard, John Taylor, Hazel Aird, Dr. Raymond Miller, Hazel Mills, Marquis Shattuck, Dr. Alfred Whittaker, Mabel Smith, Thomas Leadbetter, Charles Delbridge Jr., Gracie Krum, Brewster Campbell, Mary Murphy, George Stark, Gustave Wellensick, and Prentiss Brown. Photo by Press-Publicity Commercial Photography, Detroit.

grand and traditional fashion—with a celebratory dinner at the Park Shelton Hotel. During the program, George Stark retired from the commission to huge accolades. He died nineteen days later.

Simons assumed the presidency of the Historical Commission. Hazen Kunz, who replaced Donald Kiskadden, stepped up to the vice presidency, and Margaret (Mrs. Gerald) Slattery replaced Hazel Mills. Alfred Pelham, with deep roots in Detroit's African American community, filled the spot vacated by Stark. Frank Woodford was announced as Stark's replacement as City Historiographer although his tenure was short; he died the following summer. Monsignor Edward Hickey, a Society trustee since 1928, was appointed historiographer in 1967.

The spring also greeted announcements that the DeRoy donation, mentioned earlier, had been accepted for the Dossin Great Lakes Museum expansion, and the Gothic Room would be open by midsummer. Additionally, the City

Soon after the *J. T. Wing* was destroyed in 1956, Roy Dossin (left) presents George Stark his letter of commitment to help finance a new maritime museum as Leonard Simons looks on.

In a 1964 gathering, Sebastian Kresge tenders his letter of financial support for a Detroit Historical Museum expansion to Detroit Mayor Jerome Cavanagh, as trustees and commissioners look on. They include (left to right) Hazen Kunz, Henry Brown, George Stark, Leonard Simons, Amos Gregory (Kresge Foundation), Gordon Rice, and DHS President Paul L. Penfield.

Commissioners and Historical Department staff join Frank Woodford (second from left) after he is sworn in as City Historiographer in 1966. They include (left to right) Hazen Kunz, Thomas Leadbetter, Henry Brown, and Bartlett Frost.

Museums Director Solon Weeks receives a certificate from Detroit City Councilman Rev. John W. Peoples in 1972 as trustee Dr. Philip Mason looks on.

Museums Director Barry Dressel with Judith Dressel, Beryl Winkleman, and Leonard Simons at the Christmas Gala held at the Wayne County Building, newly renovated in 1988.

Museums Director Maud Lyon joins a guest at the 1990 Christmas party.

This 2002 gathering includes DHS President Kevin Broderick, retiring DHS Executive Director Dick Strowger, past President Mary Lou Zieve, and past Detroit Historical Commission President John Booth II.

Captured at a 1950s-themed party in the "Streets of Old Detroit" in 2005 are (left to right) Mimi McMillan, DHS trustee Sandy McMillan, Mary Ann Bury, DHS Executive Director Bob Bury, Ann Zembala, and Museums Director Dennis Zembala.

DHS Executive Director Bob Bury, trustee Rick Ruffner, and DHS President Tom Buhl in 2014.

was seeking the remaining seventy acres at old Fort Wayne for a heritage park. Planning for the Kresge Exhibition Hall wing on Kirby Street was well underway. In anticipation, museum and Society staff relocated to new office spaces on the museum's third floor.

On September 26, ground was broken for this second phase, being designed by Kapp's firm, Smith, Hinchman and Grylls. The new 21,000-square-foot Kresge wing was designed for education, with a separate entrance on Kirby to accommodate school groups and meeting attendees. The 1900-period extension of the "Streets of Old Detroit" would accompany an auditorium and exhibition space on the lower level, with large exhibition galleries and meeting rooms on the first and second floors and offices above. The addition would be completed in 1968.

In the meantime, during the hot summer of 1967, Detroit experienced the nation's worst urban rebellion of modern times. Among dozens that year throughout the country, and generally referred to locally as the "Riots," this event was the result of decades of frustration within the African American community resulting from overt racism, particularly related to the Detroit Police Department. Despite efforts within Mayor Jerome Cavanagh's administration to address the issues, anger erupted into looting and confrontation in July. Detroiters, both Black and White, reacted in ways that adversely affected the city for generations, despite some well-intentioned efforts.

The Detroit Historical Society responded in mostly positive but limited ways. The staff had included African Americans since the early 1950s, generally as preparators, tour guides, clerical staff, and maintenance. In a 1951 staff photo, seven of the twenty-eight included are Black. After 1967, their presence was noted with increased frequency in the *Bulletin*'s "Who's Who" section, but Blacks were not represented in the higher echelons of management, a situation that did not change for many years. In an editorial highly reflective of the times, Dr. Miller posited that "injustice and prejudice and discrimination are indefensible." But he added defensively that "cities don't deserve blame for everything." The editorial bore much truth, stated in Miller's straightforward style, but reflected an entrenched perspective shared by fewer and fewer Detroiters.

The Detroit Historical Museum, through its first seventeen years, had numerous exhibitions and lectures about various ethnic groups, including at least two on "Negros" in Detroit. In the fall of 1967, the Museums Department partnered with the International Afro-American Museum and founder Charles Wright to create a traveling exhibition that could easily reach schools in Detroit's vast neighborhoods. The first of three stated goals was "To give an accurate sense of identity and worth to America's Negro citizens by demonstrating the quality and depth of their contributions to world culture, and particularly to the New World"—a goal still realized today at the Charles H. Wright Museum of African American History, or more succinctly, the Wright Museum.

The Michigan Council for the Arts (today the Michigan Council for Arts and Cultural Affairs) gifted matching funds for the traveling museum. At the Michigan State Fair that year, almost 20,000 people visited. Additionally, the Detroit Historical Museum recognized Negro History Week, launched in 1926 by Carter Woodson of Howard University, for the first time in 1968.

Another initiative of note was the upgrading of the museum's Education Loan Kit Program. Initially underwritten by the Guild in the 1950s, the school outreach project had grown increasingly successful to the detriment and degradation of the original kits. New packages were created covering ten topics ranging from "Michigan Indians" to "Police" and "Fire," and containing appropriate texts, graphics, filmstrips, and interactive materials. A few months later, the Louisa St. Clair Chapter of the DAR added funds to complete the project.

Dedication of the Kresge Exhibit Hall in 1968 was a weeklong affair that started on July 17 with a press preview. The following day, a special dinner took place with WJR's affable Bud Guest as master of ceremonies. A Detroit Historical Society member open house on July 22 was followed by the formal dedication ceremonies two days later—on July 24, of course. Seven months later William Kapp died, and a year after that Henry Brown died suddenly on February 2, 1970.

Along with George Stark's death in 1966, the passing of Henry Brown marked the end of a significant chapter in the Detroit Historical Society's story. The story was by no means over, as the leadership base remained strong, and new talent soon stepped forward. Yet this twenty-year span, with Stark and Brown leading, was arguably an apex for the Society, the Historical Commission, and the Historical Department. Together, they molded a successful business model for modern American urban history organizations, not only laying solid foundations for the future but building upon those foundations with three state-of-the-art municipally owned museums. Within those museums were scholars, educators, and public relations professionals that would personify the public history realm for years to come.

Their success was partly attributable to the postwar period, when patriotism and reflection on the "American Way" were also peaking. Although managing three historical facilities did not prove sustainable under the original model, the dissimilar but dynamic personalities of Stark and Brown, and their obvious dedication to Detroit, drove the Society into the next era.

# CHAPTER THREE

# DRIVING TOWARD A NEW MILLENNIUM

It's a good thing the Society stayed in that wing on the top floor
of the Historical Museum, and that relationship continued.

—MAUD MARGARET LYON, DIRECTOR OF
THE DETROIT HISTORICAL DEPARTMENT

THE previous two decades were the building phase for Detroit's historical triumvirate. The next three decades would see maturation as the partners defined their roles. The welcoming and informational elements of the mission were primary, but together each organization would have to deal with dramatic reductions in resources, significant changes in educational methodologies and exhibit philosophies, and incredible shifts in the demographics of their constituencies. Each would also benefit from many creative young staffers, enthusiastic support from internal affinity groups and longtime partners, and significant investments in hallmark permanent and temporary exhibitions. While not always rosy, this era reflected the gutsy dedication, imagination, and optimism found in pride of purpose.

In a healthy manner, change happened slowly. There was no immediate shift in programming or exhibit philosophy. It is easy to see, reviewing the issues of the *Bulletin*, a familiar, intractable "we've always done it this way" attitude plodding on. The very European Christian Christmas Open House continued, with nods to Latin America and "emerging African nations." This was the norm and not as out of place as it sounds fifty years later, as the regional population remained overwhelmingly Christian, although the percentage of Europeans was gradually shrinking. Detroit's sizable Jewish population and nascent Muslim population did not have a similar holiday presence in the museum.

In 1970, the Black Historic Sites Committee, chaired by Detroit Councilman Ernest C. Browne Jr., was formed to research and identify significant sources and locations of civic pride in the African American community. The Senior Citizen's Arts and Crafts Exhibit continued to grow. The Patriot Assembly, Teacher of the Month, Policeman of the Month, Indian-Pilgrim Dinner, and Guild fashion shows remained part of the annual calendar for much of the next decade.

There were some notable new elements. Increasingly, national topics like space exploration and advancements in energy and communication sciences were featured in exhibits on Woodward—presumably with some great local content—and popular topics at the Dossin included underwater exploration, preserving the commercial maritime, and powerboat racing.

## IN A NEW DIRECTION

Before progressing any further, the organization needed a new leader, and a search commenced, as soon as appropriate, following Brown's death. As mentioned previously, the leadership ranks were strong, with Mark Stevens as Society president, guided by experienced trustees like Harold Hastings, Marquis Shattuck, and Thomas Leadbetter, as well as talented newcomers like Arthur Johnson and Philip Mason. Barbara Nolan, long-time executive secretary, would soon pass the torch to her assistant, Beatrice Jobagy, who remained a significant presence through the 1990s. Richard Witkowski had overseen accounting needs since the early 1950s. On the museum side, Assistant Director Bartlett Frost departed about this time, and Glenn Stille followed at the end of 1971 to become director of the Fort Snelling Museum in Minnesota. Veteran curators Margot Pearsall and Bob Lee remained.

Detroit-born Solan Weeks, chosen by the Historical Commission, was announced as the new coordinating director of museums by Mayor Roman Gribbs on August 24, 1970. It was a natural fit. With education degrees from Wayne University, his master of arts thesis was titled "The Detroit Historical Museum: Its Heritage, History and New Horizon." His first museum job was with the Historical Department, curating industrial history and education and managing the relationship with educational broadcaster WTVS. From 1960 to 1966, he served as director of the Michigan Historical Commission Museum (today the Michigan History Museum), before moving to Old Sturbridge Village in Massachusetts.

The November *Bulletin* carried his first editorial, titled "A New Voice," in which Weeks said that, "having enjoyed the great privilege of working under his direction," he knew that filling Brown's shoes could not be done. He continued, "I came to realize that there would certainly be a distinct advantage to all concerned if someone who had previously worked under his direction and who understood and appreciated his philosophy about the role of urban museums and historical societies in our contemporary society could step in and pick up the reins."

He closed by citing the tight relationship between the Detroit Historical Commission and the Detroit Historical Society and anticipating working closely with everyone moving forward.

One of the first exhibits to open on Weeks's watch was a celebration of the 50th anniversary of radio station WWJ-AM, among the first commercial transmitters in North America and the first to offer scheduled programming. Among the positive outcomes of this exhibit were significant donations of early radio equipment from WWJ with curatorial input from Edwin Boyes, a long-time engineer there, which nicely complemented material from radio pioneer Thomas E. Clark, received in the early 1950s.

What followed was "Detroit—City of the '70s," an exhibition that opened to great fanfare on January 27, 1971, featuring numerous examples of people envisioning Detroit in the future. The Exhibit Opening program, led by Mayor Roman Gribbs, included a surprise presentation to Leonard Simons of the City of Detroit Medallion in honor of his twenty-five years of service to the Historical Commission.

In preparation for the Society's 50th anniversary, the "Historymobile" school bus project was launched, intended to provide transportation for students to the museums. This was part of a broader Education Division initiative in 1971 that included adult antique restoration workshops, a "Drop in the Bucket" three-day camp for ninety children in June, and a children's parade held in conjunction with the Detroit-Windsor International Freedom Festival on July 4. Later in the summer, "Then Again" workshops introduced children to hands-on activities like weaving, stenciling, and printing, and on Fridays, storytellers from the Detroit Public Library held artifact drawing sessions at the museum. The former Education Hall on the lower level was reimagined as the Discovery Center.

Another move aimed at elevating the Society's contribution to scholarship was led by long-time trustee and chair of the Research and Publications Committee, Dr. Raymond Miller. The result was *Detroit in Perspective: A Journal of Regional History*, "a formal journal of appropriate distinction." In describing the need for such a volume, Miller wrote, "Our comprehension today tends to be distorted by the dominance of things contemporary. Time, relevance, and sequence collapse when we can watch Olympic games as they are run, when we can send a man to the moon in the time it took our grandfather to get to the state capital, and when the entire world pours at us, hourly, frantic accounts of undetermined import. We suffer from the oppressive pressure of the present." One wonders what he would say about the world fifty years later!

Launched in autumn 1972, and published also in winter and spring, each issue of the journal featured three or four peer-reviewed professional papers. The initial editor was W. Sprague Holden, a former newspaperman who then chaired the Journalism Department at Wayne State University. While the *Journal* was a boon to serious students of regional history, the *Bulletin* had been the diary of the Society—a view into life of a leading museum, describing its staff, its exhibitions, its membership and donors, and the wishes and dreams of its leaders. To future students of museology, the loss of the *Bulletin* was significant. The final issue was published in December 1971.

Dr. Philip Mason of the Department of History at Wayne State University began editing the *Journal* starting with the winter 1975 edition. He was succeeded by Kermit Hall in 1978 and JoEllen Vinyard in spring 1982. Budget cuts caused suspension of *Detroit in Perspective* in the fall of 1983.

Changes in the national economy in the 1970s and 1980s had a direct impact on the city and its historical society. In 1960, nearly every car in North America was built in Michigan or Ontario. Two decades later, fuel-efficient foreign automobiles challenged Detroit's Big Three at a time when gasoline prices were being adversely affected by international politics. In the Great Lakes region, this affected every sector of the economy from mining and shipping to tax revenues and education. Southeastern Michigan was doubly stunned when auto manufacturing was moved to cheap-labor southern states and Mexico. International war and political intrigues were daily television fare. By the mid-1980s, the deindustrialization of Detroit was nearly complete, and it caught many by surprise.

What was widely acknowledged was the dramatic shift of people and businesses out of the city. "White flight" was not a new phenomenon; it started soon after World War II but accelerated through the 1990s. In 1960, Detroit had 1,670,000 people, 70 percent of them White. In 1990, Detroit had just over a million residents, and 75 percent of them were Black. The core city saw a dramatic rise in commercial vacancies. Even as significant renewal projects were underway—Renaissance Center, Orchestra Hall, Fox Theatre—anchor retailers like Hudson's, Grinnell Brothers, and Wright-Kay closed their doors. The cumulative effect on tax revenues, which supported Historical Department initiatives, was stunning.

Cuts to the museum budgets resulted in some creative, mission-related efforts that raised funds and improved preservation. There were also some significant distractions that spread resources thin. In the first category, commission president Barbara Wrigley and Guild leaders Dorothea Hibbler and Cynthia Young created the first "Attic Sale" at Historic Fort Wayne, which raised $18,000 and was the basis for a flea market that was held twice-yearly through 2019. The Historymobile program not only got students to the museums but facilitated the Historic Church tours and other outreach events. The Historical Department reorganized its accounting process, and staffing at both the department and Society remained slim. The Society's Historic Preservation Committee undertook a review of historic sites for nomination to the National Register of Historic Places.

But the distractions were many. The Moross House, Detroit's oldest brick building, underwent a complete restoration and was then leased to the Detroit Garden Center. At some point, the Palmer Log Cabin in Palmer Park was managed by the Historical Department, although it is never mentioned in the literature until after its closure due to vandalism. Trustees finally organized the tour of "Cadillac's Homeland" for twenty-three members focused on dedication events at his newly restored birthplace at St. Nicolas de la Grave, a restoration partially underwritten by Society donors. The commission and Society were caught up in planning for the nation's bicentennial in 1976, and while the *Journal* project was admirable, it had a narrow appeal and ongoing expenses.

By far, the greatest attention was focused on the incredible opportunity offered by Historic Fort Wayne. By the 1970s, the roughly 50 riverfront acres controlled by the City surrounding the "Fort Wayne Military Museum" had been rebranded as "Historic Fort Wayne." An initiative led by Curator Dr. William Phenix was designed to upgrade the visitor experience through a revamped Interpretive Center, a new Woodland Indian Interpretive Center, and a broad reimagining of the entire campus. The estimated cost to demolish World War II parade ground warehouses, remove asphalt from inside the fort, and reconstruct the fort's earthworks was pegged at $2.5 million, largely paid for through Community Development Block Grant Funds. On May 10, 1986, the U.S. Interior Department gave Detroit an additional 30 acres of fort property; it now owned everything except the 15-acre parcel retained by the Army Corps of Engineers. Over the next several years, millions of dollars were spent to upgrade electrical and security services, pave a large parking lot, add period lighting around the fort, light the parade grounds, restore the 1880s Commanding Officer's home, upgrade fabrication workshops and a business center, repurpose three old warehouses into a modern collections facility, and maintain a corps of fifteen costumed reenactors as visitor guides.

This aerial photograph of the campus at Historic Fort Wayne shows the new parking lot in the foreground and the parade ground clear of all World War II–era warehouses in 1979.

In the grand scheme, the fort property was meant to become a nationally significant tourist attraction. Indeed, in 1974, Family Day (alternately called Frontier Day and later Fort Wayne Days) drew 6,000 visitors, and a traveling exhibition from the Smithsonian Institution of Revolutionary War documents drew 7,000. But this should be put in context.

In December 1975, cuts to City budgets forced the Dossin Great Lakes Museum to close its doors. The Detroit Historical Museum and Historic Fort Wayne were shuttered in April 1976. The Clark Endowment, which stood at over $100,000 in 1969, had shrunk to a few thousand dollars. Only an emergency allocation of $700,000 by the Michigan state legislature allowed the facilities to reopen. The Dossin was unlocked on June 10, thanks to a grant from Helen DeRoy, and the Woodward museum opened again on July 6—two days after the huge bicentennial celebrations. Fort Wayne opened for a single day—June 11—to celebrate the 180th anniversary of Detroit becoming an American town in 1796.

Despite this, work at Fort Wayne continued. At the Dossin museum, the only event noted in the 1976 annual report was an exhibition and publication based on Karl Kuttruff's illustrations called *Great Lakes Ships: A Bicentennial*

*Exhibit*, commissioned by the Great Lakes Maritime Institute and published with Guild funds.

At the Detroit Historical Museum, the scene was a scramble. According to Weeks, when the museum "reopened its doors in July, a number of exhibit halls were empty, and a frantic effort was made to get the changing exhibit program back on schedule." From July 1976 through April 1977, twenty-five changing exhibits were installed, including the fourth and fifth versions of "Documenting Detroit"—produced in collaboration with the photography department of the College for Creative Studies—three traveling exhibitions, three African American–oriented displays, a baseball exhibit, and the "Collector's Corner" featuring antique crystal knife holders. Staff—now up to seventy-four at the three facilities—somehow found time to generate the traveling exhibition "Symbols of a New Nation" that only traveled to three venues—another distraction.

Programming was equally frenetic, hosting dozens of free workshops, a statewide dulcimer convening, and a Wednesday evening concert series. Noel Night drew 6,000 people. During Afro-American History month in 1977, trustee Ann Thompson spearheaded "Heritage of Black Music" with live performances and the majority of attendees in traditional African dress. Monthly Historic Church tours continued to sell out well in advance.

August saw the retirement of Assistant Director Margot Pearsall after a career of almost thirty years. Mayoral appointee Alma Stallworth, the deputy director, resigned in July 1978 and was replaced by Betty Allen.

## BUILDING MOMENTUM

While things settled down a bit the following fiscal year, money was still tight. In his 1978 president's report, Hudson Mead called out the "Society's seeming inability to obtain major gifts from individuals," citing it as a top priority going forward. Director Weeks's 1979 report indicates that contributions to the roughly $2.2 million budget came from the City (45 percent), state (34 percent), and Federal Comprehensive Employment and Training Act (19 percent, for twenty-nine staff), and earned revenue from admissions and program fees (2 percent). On top of this, the City provided Fort Wayne restoration with $1,000,000 in bond funds and $91,000 in block grant funding. The Society and Guild donated $45,300. The following year, the Kresge Foundation provided $150,000 to complete renovation and furnishing of the Commander's House, a project directed by museum curators James Conway and Cynthia Young, assisted and subsidized by the Michigan chapter of the National Society of the Colonial Dames. The completed house museum opened to Fort Wayne visitors in 1986.

Exhibitions at the Woodward museum included yearlong installations of "Detroit's African-American Heritage" and "Dressed in Detroit: Detroit Stores and Their Fashions—1890–1950," as well as a Detroit Historical Society 50th Anniversary salute. The Dossin had showings for three marine artists and a Belle Isle Park centennial. Programming was much as the year before and included a presentation of historic dolls by registrar Patience Nauta. The Black Historic Sites Committee installed five new historical markers, bringing their total to fifteen. Among the 437 objects donated to the collection in 1978–79 was a legendary gift from Robert Byrne of five Indy racing cars valued at $82,500. These would be sold in 1992 for $153,000 to fund other accessions.

From an operational standpoint, a few forward-thinking, strategic changes occurred during this decade. Committees of the Board of Trustees now numbered fourteen, down from twenty-six two decades earlier. More important, in 1959, twenty of the committees were designated "special," dealing with everything from lecture schedules and maritime matters to various special events and oral history collections. In 1979, the eight special committees were strategically focused on legal and government relations, marketing, and corporate contributions. Only the Audio-Visual and Research-Publications committees were mission-related. Society staff remained at four, although at least a dozen or more City employees were contracted through the Society.

Membership stood at 1,900 in 1978, markedly down from the peak of 3,382 in 1952. To address this decline, membership levels were reorganized in categories more familiar today: life, honorary, donor, sustaining, family, individual, and student levels. The business founders level was gone, although a corporate giving category reappeared a few years later.

The Historical Commission, chaired by Charles Hagler, at this time included historian Dr. Norman McRae, financial wizard Alfred Pelham—both important African American voices—former DHS Guild President Margaret Slattery, and Barbara Wrigley. The Society had also created an Advisory Council made up of seven past presidents. In addition to the Society president, there was now a paid executive director to handle Society business full-time. Nancy Cunningham filled this role starting in 1977.

The 1980s began with a slightly better outlook. Despite the rather dour observation from Society President Henry Earle that the organization was "not yet one of the region's 'priority agencies,'" Solan Weeks's budget report for 1980 shows the total allocation for the year up 33 percent from the year before to $2,850,000. Donations from the Society to the Historical Department more than tripled to $150,000. As the economy goes, so goes the Society. Manufacturing rebounded and a semblance of social stability through the 1980s caused the fortunes of both the City and the organization to improve. However, while public funding for the historical museums and other cultural organizations had increased from 1950 to the 1970s, the tide now shifted toward a greater reliance upon private support as government budgets continued to shrink.

The next couple of years are not well documented. It is assumed that, in general, the Historical Department lumbered ahead in its three separate locations, with separate staffs and divergently different budgets. Because of its size and needs, Historic Fort Wayne absorbed the lion's share of annual allocations; the Dossin Great Lakes Museum received very little. Local newspapers were full of schedules for neighborhood strolls and Historic Church tours. The Society sponsored a conference called "The Automobile and American Culture" in autumn 1982. Held at Wayne State University, scholars from as far away as New York and Florida came, without compensation, to share their thoughts and research.

Notable milestones included a Christmas Dinner Dance, which was added to holiday activities in 1981 and became the Society's signature fundraising event. The vast train collection of Alfred Glancy, donated in 1971, became a traditional treat during the holidays. The permanent track layout installed in 1981 was an instant hit. In February 1982, the Detroit Historical Society Guild presented its 30th Patriotic Award to Walter Green. Originally part of Patriot Day celebrations in the 1950s, that event—once a grand spectacle—had ceased a decade earlier but the award lived on.

Tragedy struck in October 1984 when Solan Weeks succumbed to lymphatic cancer at Harper Hospital. He had struggled with it for six years and valiantly kept his hand on the helm through the ordeal. Jim Conway, architectural history curator for the Historical Department, stated, "Solan Weeks was beloved by the museum staff, Commissioners, and Detroit Historical Society Trustees, and was deeply respected" within the public history community. Mayor Coleman Young's statement read, "Solan Weeks loved this city and its history, and devoted his life to assuring that history was preserved." Sadly, his wife, Patricia, had to sue the City for his pension, withheld over a technicality. She lost on appeal.

Deputy Director Betty Allen managed the department until a nationwide search resulted in the hiring of Barry Dressel, formerly vice president of the City Life Museums of Baltimore, in the autumn of 1985. In his first public report—a Historical Department–only annual report published after his first year on the job—he highlighted some of the advantages and challenges facing the public history organizations in Detroit. On the plus side, he inherited several good things "that other historical agencies don't enjoy": solid attendance, active support groups, good facilities, a large collection, half of the fifty-member staff dedicated to mission-related activities, and a steady stream of funding from the city and state.

The issues were more numerous, and four in particular stood out to Dressel. First, his interpretation of the 1973 master plan for Historic Fort Wayne suggested that it "cannot ever receive adequate funding for implementation. The visitation levels and operating costs could not thereafter justify the original investment." (One commentator suggested that the fort was "an oasis of serenity surrounded by deferred maintenance.") Second, he noted that while storage space at Fort Wayne was nearly unlimited, the sheer "number of areas defeated any effort to raise them to an acceptable level of quality," and without a coherent plan "the Department collected almost anything offered." Third was that "exhibits tend to be temporary, low-budget affairs, greeted with tepid interest by the media and the public." Educational programming was also poorly coordinated and promoted. Finally, the overall management structure was inefficient, absorbing upper management in day-to-day operations as opposed to strategic and financial direction. He also suggested that the Historical Department's relationship with the Society had been neglected for several years and recognized that the Historical Commission had been severely marginalized by the City.

His first major change was to create a new management hierarchy with dedicated staff coordinating functionality at all departmental locations as related to collections, interpretation, marketing, and curation. Interpretive plans for Historic Fort Wayne and the Detroit Historical Museum were discarded, "saving $25M worth of fiscally imprudent projects." Interpretation at Historic Fort Wayne was concentrated on "living history" at the star fort, while other buildings were reevaluated. Plans for the Collections Resource Center were upgraded to include office space so that "for the first time in 40 years the collections and curators will be housed in the same location."

The Woodward museum was to concentrate on quality, long-term exhibit installations. The Costume Gallery would be the first beneficiary of an agreement with the Society to secure funding from within the business community. "A colorful, relevant history of Detroit, presented with style and sympathy, wit and scholarship, is the ultimate solution to unmet potential," Dressel opined. Representing a strategic switch, large galleries were to have the long-term exhibits, with small spaces hosting the temporary ones.

Notably, nowhere in his report does he mention the Dossin Great Lakes Museum, reflecting its place in the shadows of the fort and Woodward museum. This is a curious omission since Dressel's doctorate from the University of Delaware in museum studies had a maritime history focus. While accounting for 24 percent of the Historical Department's annual attendance, the Belle Isle museum received very little City funding beyond staff and groundskeeping. Bob Lee retired in 1980, replaced by transportation curator John Polacsek, who enjoyed a twenty-five-year tenure. In 1986, new gallery lighting was purchased and installed by the Great Lakes Maritime Institute, and fresh signage came through a grant from the International Shipmasters Association. Admission fees from a model ship contest and revenues produced by a maritime antiques market, along with support from the scuba diving community, resulted in an exhibition called "Maritime Time Capsules" and an accompanying gallery guide.

Up on Woodward, the big hit in 1986 was "UAW's First 50 Years: Economic Progress and Social Justice." This project included an exhibition, lectures, and a live performance created by union members based on their factory experiences. Accompanied by four small auto-related exhibits, over 70,000 visitors participated in various activities. Ironically, a citywide strike in July by 7,000 members of Detroit's Council 25 of the American Federation of State, County and Municipal Employees, representing unionized museum greeters, guards, and maintenance staff, closed the Historical Department's three facilities for twenty days.

During that year, the museum hosted complementary installations titled "The History of Women in Michigan" and "Black Women in Michigan: 1785–1985." The Social History Division created exhibits on toys and quilts, the latter being part of the Michigan quilting inventory project. At the fort, a vintage car show, the Guild's flea market, Civil War Days, and annual Indian powwow drew about half of the fort's 15,000 annual attendees—about 6 percent of the departmental total. Progress on the collections facility and the National Museum of the Tuskegee Airmen was underway.

By 1988, new executive leadership, including Commission President Barbara Wrigley, Society President Philip Moon, and Executive Director Michael W. R. Davis, energetically supported Dressel's agenda. An important part of his strategy was to create greater transparency between the three historical agencies. The underlying issue was a general distrust of City government in the private sector, and the Society was no exception. Trustees considered that if the City knew how much money the Society was contributing to the museums the City would simply cut its part of the budget. Dressel convinced them—private sector trustees and public sector financial staff—to share information so that everyone understood what the true budget of the historical museums was and where it came from. For the first time ever, the Historical Commission, Historical Department, and Society released a joint annual report, reflecting the greater degree of cooperation demanded by Dressel. It was an important step toward increasing trust and teamwork and continued for many years.

Partnerships became key to new exhibition initiatives. The new Booth-Wilkinson Costume Gallery on the second floor, which opened with "The 7

Ages of Women" exhibit in November 1987, as well as the adjoining Tavy Stone Fashion Library, got significant funding and support from the local chapter of the Fashion Group, as well as the Gannett, McGregor, and M. R. Wilson foundations. This dual project covered 4,000 square feet with an initial cost of $260,000 to refit the space.

The exciting new "Selling American Dreams: The Marketing of the Motor-car" was popular from October 1986 through January 1987 and received support from *Automotive News*, Ford Motor Company, and J. Walter Thompson advertising. On the first floor, the Museum of American Folk Art in New York brought in the patriotic exhibit "Liberties with Liberty." Stark Hall was renovated as a changing exhibition space and opened with "Artists of Michigan from the Nineteenth Century," a GTE touring exhibit. The partnership with the Guild on the "Old Detroit Shop" resulted in a handsome new retail facility located in the middle of Round Hall. "Iron Men and Steel Vessels: The History of the Great Lakes Engineering Works" at the Dossin and the Tuskegee Airmen museum at Historic Fort Wayne received support from their respective affinity groups.

Such partnerships were generating plans for a revitalized Kresge Educational Wing and complete reimagining of Dodge Hall as a permanent, automotive exhibition. Updates at the Dossin were also in the works, even as the first phase of the collections building at Historic Fort Wayne was being completed in 1989. These rapid changes were in process as Barry Dressel's time in Detroit ended. That year he accepted a position at the Berkshire Museum in Massachusetts. Nine years later, after a stint at the Turks and Caicos National Museum in the British West Indies, he returned to the area as director of the Walter P. Chrysler Museum and Heritage Center in Auburn Hills.

Directorship of the Historical Department was then vested in Chief Curator Maud Margaret Lyon in 1990. Despite severe cuts in state budget allocations—then the Historical Department's largest source of funding—Lyon was able to maintain Dressel's momentum through the next decade. She noted in a recent interview that Society trustees discussed severing ties with the Historical Department at this juncture, but Society President John L. Booth II convinced them to stay the course. Booth's leadership, both as a donor and later as president of the Historical Commission, preserved the relationship that ultimately kept the museums operating.

Through this era, the Society board included many stalwarts: Barbara Wrigley, Norman McRae, Dwight Vincent, Sue Vititoe, Warren Wilkinson, George Johnson, and Mary Lou Zieve (Leonard Simons's daughter). Both Wrigley and Wilkinson served as leaders of the Historical Commission, bringing insight to an increasingly titular City entity. There were also some newer members who would have an impact in years to come, including Kevin Broderick, Doug Dossin (Russell Dossin's grandson), Judy Christie, and John Stroh III.

The highest-profile victims of shrinking allocations were Dressel's newly hired, young professional staff who left for other opportunities and Historic Fort Wayne, which was closed to the public in 1991. Despite this, the Historical Department stayed on course with the new direction designed to improve collections management and upgrade exhibitions at the Detroit Historical Museum and Dossin Great Lakes Museum. The exhibit fabrication shop remained in operation and a second phase of the Collections Resource Center was underway, even while overall staff positions within the Historical Department were reduced by 40 percent, mostly at Historic Fort Wayne. Society administrative staff remained at six.

Another sign of the times was that in the summer of 1992, many of the temporary exhibitions installed in 1988 were still active, including "Collectors in Toyland," "Pressing Matters" (about a woman's battle against wrinkled clothes), and "Under the Skin: The Changing Anatomy of American Cars."

Book fairs in Dodge Hall, like this one in 1956, would draw thousands of students and families over several weeks.

Children wave from the windows of the Detroit Historical Society's Historymobile in 1968.

StoryLiving troupe included (front, left to right) Sakunah Delaney, founder Randi Douglas, Stefan Kukurugya; (rear, left to right) Jim Perkins, Robert Jones, Gillian Eaton, Josh White Jr., and Karen Burr.

Docent Sadie Brown leads a school group tour of "Frontiers to Factories" in 1998.

New was "Striving to Succeed: African American Businessmen in Detroit." Also new was a successful StoryLiving program founded by Randi Douglas and funded by the Detroit Historical Society to increase educational programming. Designed to take Detroit culture into schools at a time when schools could no longer afford field trips to the museum, this intimate performance format used music and theater to engage children in history. StoryLiving featured some of the finest local artists, including Robert Jones, Josh White Jr., Sakunah Delaney, Karen Burr, Jim Perkins, Stefan Kukurugya, and Gillian Eaton.

Planning for the future "Motor City" exhibition continued, thanks in part to a $50,000 grant from the National Endowment for the Humanities that allowed design and curatorial development to continue behind the scenes. Exhibits that opened to the public in the early 1990s included installations in the second-level costume gallery and fashion library. The first level featured an update of the 1987 exhibit "Outposts to Industries," retitled "Furs to Factories: Detroit at Work, 1701–1901," designed by Ken Osen and Curator Bill Phenix, which opened at the end of 1992. A 140-seat theater (later the Louise C. Booth Auditorium), an upgraded Glancy Trains layout, and a long-term toy exhibit occupied the western lower level. The *Detroit Free Press* described the initiatives as "creativity that transcends budget cuts and staff reductions."

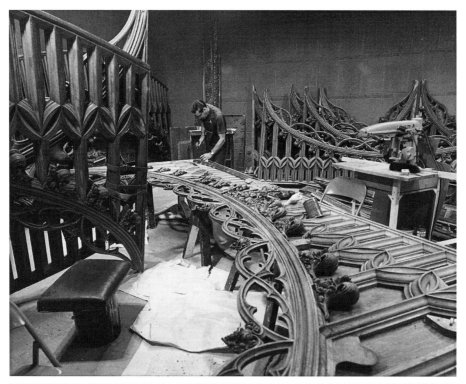

Restoration of the *City of Detroit III*'s Gothic Room in process, under the skilled hands of museum preparator Paul Coletta. 1965. *Detroit Free Press* photograph.

The starboard bow anchor, left behind by the S.S. *Edmund Fitzgerald* in 1974, is recovered from the Detroit River before being put on permanent display at the Dossin Great Lakes Museum. 1992.

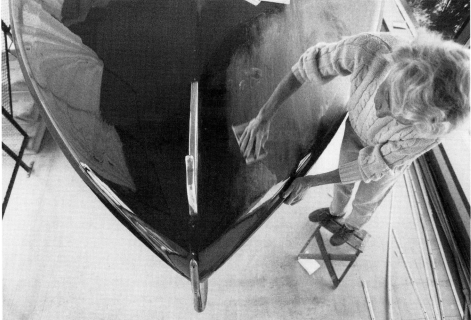

A barge approaches the Dossin Great Lakes Museum with the pilothouse from the freighter S.S. *William Clay Ford*. 1991.

Volunteer Peggy Breck is hard at work restoring the mahogany hull of the hydroplane *Miss Pepsi*. 1991.

Equally impressive were the artifact recovery projects instituted at the Dossin Great Lakes Museum. Curator John Polacsek's relationships with energetic affinity groups resulted in several high-profile acquisitions in the early 1990s. The following were supported financially and logistically by GLMI, the International Shipmasters Association (ISMA), and the Detroit Police Department's Underwater Recovery Team, as well as companies like Faust Engineering, Gaelic Tugs, Diamond Jack Tours, and WDIV-TV.

Of greatest impact was installation of the S.S. *William Clay Ford*'s pilothouse on the river side of the building. The *Ford*, retired in 1986, carried some notoriety as one of the vessels that left Whitefish Bay in 1975 to search for the ill-fated S.S. *Edmund Fitzgerald*. As the most recent of the Great Lakes shipwrecks, and made famous by a hit radio ballad, the *Fitzgerald* became known around the world. When the *Ford* was scrapped, the salvor, E. Stephen Robinson of Ervin Robinson Company, preserved the pilothouse, and it was donated to the museum. GLMI supplied funding for the infrastructure.

The original Dossin building was designed with upper and lower indoor observation decks on the river. This allowed the *Ford*'s pilothouse to be installed adjacent to the upper level, with the captain's stairs leading down to an interpretive level below. Through 1989 and 1990, plans were developed and permits were pulled. Ground was broken on July 24, 1990, and foundation work continued through the summer.

On April 3, 1991, a tug and barge loaded with the pilothouse and a crane worked its way upriver from the Rouge River and nudged up to the Dossin's breakwall. Another crane waited onshore, and the two lifted the artifact onto its new base, ready for sealing and wiring. The impressive addition was officially opened to the public with great fanfare on March 6, 1992. This massive artifact was a perfect bookend to the Gothic Room, representing two beautifully preserved—and relatively kid-proof—experiential pieces of Great Lakes history.

Compared to this extensive project, the next two adventures seem less complicated but were neither simple—for both were underwater—nor less historic. In late July 1991, a team of divers, informally known as the Dossin Dive Team, recovered most of a 23-foot runabout from the Detroit River west of the Belle Isle Bridge. Evidence aboard the craft suggested that the boat carried illegal beer during Prohibition and was scuttled by its pilot to avoid arrest. Sadly, the wood of the craft was badly deteriorated, but the engine, controls, and cargo were included in an exhibition called "Rumrunners and Michigan's Prohibition Navy" a few years later. Almost lost among this activity was a needed restoration of *Miss Pepsi*, expertly performed by hydroplane fans led by Doug and Peggy Breck.

On May 20, 1992, members of the dive team discovered an anchor from the fabled S.S. *Edmund Fitzgerald*. The 12,290-pound starboard bow anchor was lost at the Belle Isle Anchorage east of the Renaissance Center one autumn morning in 1974. Following the loss of the *Fitz* the next year, divers began their search. After much planning, the anchor was removed from the water on July 20, 1992. Mal Sillars, a diver and popular television meteorologist on WDIV-TV, broadcast the recovery event live. Advance publicity and the popularity of *Fitzgerald* lore brought the TV station its highest ratings ever. Later, the artifact was deposited at the Dossin Great Lakes Museum, where thousands visited the anchor in the coming weeks and years.

During the middle of the decade, life for Maud Lyon's team was a roller coaster. Reduced funding from the state suddenly disappeared, even as great new programs and keystone exhibitions were being developed. Under Governor John Engler's administration, overall arts and culture funding was reduced from $29.5 million to $21.9 million, and an effort was made to distribute state arts funding more equitably statewide through the Michigan Council for the Arts and Cultural Affairs (MCACA). This resulted in a smaller portion going to cultural institutions in Detroit. The Historical Department lost 45 percent of its funding in 1995, even as the DIA and Detroit Symphony Orchestra (DSO) retained their allotments. The following year, DIA funding was cut by 15 percent, the DSO lost 7 percent, and the historical museums received under $1 million—a 75 percent cut from only a few years prior. At the same time, the Music Hall, Center for Creative Studies, Museum of African American History, Michigan Opera Theatre, and Edison Institute saw modest state funding increases.

## MOTOR CITY MAGIC

In reaction to the 1995 cuts, the Kresge Foundation came forward with a $400,000 challenge grant to jump-start donations for the "Motor City" educational goal, a campaign dubbed "History in the Making: Funding for Education," led by Warren Wilkinson. It was the most ambitious fundraising campaign of the Detroit Historical Society since the 1951 construction of the Detroit Historical Museum. John Booth and Bud Marx, grandson of Oscar Marx (Detroit mayor, 1913–18), also played major roles in the campaign.

Anticipating the centenary of Detroit's automobile industry in 1996, dozens of regional auto suppliers stepped forward with money—ultimately $4.3 million—and artifacts to fund a $2 million installation and staff for broader educational initiatives. The project entailed a fantastic reimagining of the museum's largest gallery. Dodge Hall's 8,000-square-foot, two-story expanse was the building's show space, formerly hosting auto exhibits, Christmas tree fundraisers, book fairs, performances, flower shows, and special temporary exhibitions.

With Society funding, it now became a permanent paean to the auto industry called the "Motor City" exhibition.

With the replica of Charles Brady King's first car as a starting point, the gallery was filled with artifacts, large and small, detailing the twin trajectories of the city and the automobile industry, and the impacts that both had on the world. By design, it addressed the businesses as well as the workers. Guest curator Mike Smith commented to the *Detroit Free Press*, "The automobile industry has always been community-based and making cars has always been a collaborative effort between the industry, the people who worked in the plants and their families."

The project opened to the public in December. At its center was a configuration of an actual "body drop" segment of the assembly line salvaged from General Motors' Cadillac Clark Street Plant in 1988. Every fifteen minutes, gongs chimed and the body of a Fleetwood sedan would be lowered to its waiting chassis below—a process developed eight decades earlier and still used in automobile manufacturing. Surrounding this showstopper were the stories of companies and families, unions and suppliers, parking meters and purpose-built factories—everything from Advertising to Ziebart.

To add to the fun, earlier in the fall the Woodward museum opened a maritime exhibition highlighting another Detroit touchstone titled "Let's Go to Boblo." This island amusement park and the "Bob-Lo Boats" that shuttled people to the downriver destination were part of Detroit's collective summer memories dating to the 1890s. When the park closed in 1993, Dossin staff and GLMI volunteers aggressively collected artifacts, and the Bob-Lo exhibit was a good draw. GLMI, described in the press as "the funding arm of the Dossin Great Lakes Museum," had initiated a major fundraising campaign to mount this exhibit. With the support of high-profile restaurateur and promoter Joe Muer, GLMI also produced the movie *Bob-Lo Memories*, published Philip Mason's *Rum Running and the Roaring Twenties* with Wayne State University Press, purchased a collection of Chris-Craft memorabilia, and held a twentieth anniversary event for the sinking of the *Edmund Fitzgerald*—precursor to the current Lost Mariners Remembrance.

On the humorous side, *Detroit News* editorial cartoonist Draper Hill got his historic moment with the exhibit "A Brush with Satire." On the sad side, the museum lost one of its founding personalities with the death of Leonard Simons in November. Among people who made things happen for the Detroit Historical Society for a very long time, Simons has few peers.

Surrounding the coming auto centennial, the Society and Historical Department planned months of events in partnership with the American Centennial Commission, Henry Ford Museum, Crain Communications' *Automotive News*,

The extensive furniture holdings at the Collections Resource Center include this cabinet carved by famed Detroit sculptor Julius Melchers around 1880.

and others. The new "Motor City" exhibition and the museum were natural venues for numerous presentations and receptions.

Just as the festivities ended, a fire destroyed the Glancy Trains Exhibit and sullied the entire lower level. It was discovered by staff on the morning of Friday, August 9, as the museum opened. Although the fire was quickly extinguished by the Detroit Fire Department, smoke damage was extensive. Of the original Glancy collection, many items were destroyed. Fortunately, as volunteer and train historian Bob Cosgrove noted, most lost items were mass-produced and easily replaced. The loss and reconstruction estimate, including a complete cleaning and restoration of the "Streets of Old Detroit," came in at $150,000. With some new interactive technologies and a spectacular new layout, Glancy Trains reopened on November 28, 1997.

The 1990s were a time when museums began to use digital technologies in exhibitions, including the use of video and interactive consoles to engage visitors. Leveraging emerging high-tech was one of the major innovations of the "Motor City" exhibition, making historical film footage and interactive exhibition components available for the first time in the museum. While the "Cadillac Body Drop" centerpiece added drama to the exhibition, it ironically celebrated a manufacturing method that was itself already being phased out of automotive manufacturing. Maintaining the body drop, a process that couldn't be replicated digitally, would be an ongoing challenge for museum staff and volunteers.

Herein lies a conundrum for archives and museums. Is the main goal preservation or education? To be best preserved, objects should not be touched or exposed to light. But the goal of a history museum is to teach, which is more effective when it is highly interactive, allowing children and adults to manipulate things to understand how they work or to explore the topic further. Balancing preservation and education requires both effective exhibitions and educational programs for the present and a robust collection management program to preserve objects for the future.

Fashion has been a focus for curators since the Society's early days, and the costume collection now numbers in the tens of thousands of items.

In the 1990s, the City's collections swelled to an estimated 135,000 items, from archives and photographs to furniture and fire trucks. Long recorded on ledgers and file cards, there was movement toward a computerized registration database. The department's long-term goal of completing a new Collections Resource Center to safely house the collection faced a major setback in 1995 when an air filtration failure caused pathogenic mold to grow in the new facility. Using funding from insurance, the museum hired a team to inspect and inventory every artifact. Starting in 2002, the process of transferring records to a PastPerfect digital database began. Almost two decades later, the data entry and inventory process is ongoing. The ledgers and 3 × 5 cards still come in handy.

Besides exhibit technologies and collection databases, computers were changing the ways in which employees communicated internally and dramatically expanded what could be printed in-house. From a public relations perspective, the earliest hints of digital marketing and social media were emerging. The operations team addressed the need for more phone lines to connect to the nascent worldwide web as well as electrical outlets and space

A group of about thirty-five vintage autos—roughly half the collection—are stored in inflatable bubbles to protect them from dust and infestation.

This coin, a double tournois from 1637, was minted in southern France and among the earliest colonial artifacts in the collection.

for the computers and printers. This seismic shift in the way business was done continued relentlessly. Coupled with drastic budget cuts, it left all City departments scrambling.

Yet, creativity and outreach were seen in the great exhibits that closed out the millennium. At the end of 1996, the museum hosted "Becoming American Women: Clothing and the Jewish Immigrant Experience, 1880–1920." A few months later, "Legacy: African American Dolls in the Victorian Era" opened through March. In the spring, "I Discover," a children's hands-on installation, was launched. By summer, the Charles H. Wright Museum of African American History moved from the New Center area to its impressive new home in the Cultural Center, a significant enhancement to the neighborhood.

In August, the Detroit Historical Museum opened "Remembering Downtown Hudson's" in recognition of the pending implosion of the iconic department store the following year. This installation generated great attendance and resulted in a number of related lectures and programs. Diverse and fun exhibits followed with "A Community Between Two Worlds" opening in March 1998 with programming, including an Arab American symposium, lasting through September. "Fantasy World of Dollhouses"—the museums had developed a spectacular collection—ran from October through January 1999. "Halloween Fun" was promoted at the museum for October 1998, a precursor to "Treats in the Streets." The "Furs to Factories" installation was remade that same year into "Frontiers to Factories." It debuted on December 9 at the Society's traditional pre-Christmas fundraiser.

As MCACA funding started to rise, eventually placing Michigan in the fourth position nationally for arts funding, operating grant funding for the Detroit Historical Department fell from $1.1 million in 1996 to $600,000 in 1997. Detroit Historical Department staff shrank to thirty-five, museum hours were reduced, and attendance gradually declined to 130,000 for the museums on Woodward and Belle Isle. It should be noted that through all the budget cuts of the 1990s, people involved in the negotiations recall that the City budget department was very helpful to the historical museums behind the scenes, absorbing deficits and finding additional funds in some lean years.

Leadership in the City's three historical entities—the commission, the department, and the Society—experienced a series of transitions. After five years as executive director of the Society, Mike Davis left in 1993, followed by three quick changes that eventually brought Richard "Dick" Strowger, a retired executive at PricewaterhouseCoopers, to the position in 1996. As a trustee, he agreed to step in as interim director and proved so effective that he was hired as executive director in April 1997.

That year, trustee Mary Lou Zieve was Society president, and former Society President John Booth headed the Historical Commission. In partnership with Booth, Lyon, and the board, Strowger was able to increase nongovernmental revenues from 15 percent to 43 percent of the overall $4.8 million budget. Strowger recalls a near-complete turnover of his eight-member staff and leveraging the openings to upgrade capabilities. He was also able to work with former colleagues in the banking sector to fund high-profile renovations of the Woodward museum in the form of BankOne Plaza. In 1998, the Society won the prestigious "Best-Managed Nonprofit" award from *Crain's Detroit Business* magazine.

Maud Lyon resigned as museums director in early 1999 to found and lead *Detroit300*, the city's tricentennial celebration. She later worked with the Detroit Symphony Orchestra and the Belle Isle Conservancy, and formed CultureSource, a regional arts and culture support coalition. Curator Vicky Kruckeberg served as interim director of the museums. Fortunately the team was strong, and the smooth transition of leadership into the early 2000s was vital to the Detroit Historical Society's survival and, in turn, survival of the City's historical museums. Stability at this time allowed a number of significant projects to be completed in preparation for the Society's next phase.

# CHAPTER FOUR

# BACK IN THE DRIVER'S SEAT

I'm confident we'll get what we need, and in the end, we will be in a better place.

—BOB BURY, EXECUTIVE DIRECTOR OF
THE DETROIT HISTORICAL SOCIETY

THE previous three decades saw misdirections, resets, and difficult financial realities, even as leadership and staff remained committed and creative. Many enduring projects were completed during the toughest times. What followed was a significant reexamination of the public-private alliance and a severe leap of faith by the Society.

In 2001, the celebration of the 300th anniversary of French traders establishing a permanent European settlement along the strait included reenactments, tall ships, parades, publications, speeches, fireworks, and exhibitions. Not long afterward, financial storm clouds grew threatening enough that the City approached the Society about assuming management control of its historical assets. In 2006, a deal was reached that included only some of the assets. The national economy crashed two years later, and two of Detroit's largest employers would enter bankruptcy, along with many smaller businesses. The City followed in 2013.

It would seem a tough time to be a museum—city-owned or not. Yet at this time, in museums across the country, the formula was being reimagined. The

Society chose a municipally owned, privately managed model that was being explored with varying degrees of success in other cities. It was new territory but proved a positive transition—depending on whom you speak to—for the museums and collections. Within a year, both museums received thorough, if superficial, buffing and polishing. Management of the collection transitioned smoothly and thrived.

It was quite a transformation, but we're getting ahead of the story. In 1999, the development and marketing departments launched the "Days of Detroit" calendar, edited by Annette and Jim McConnell and Marketing Manager Bob Sadler—a throwback to one of the Society's earliest fundraising products. The traditional Holiday Party was refashioned into the first Detroit Historical Society Ball, held at the Detroit Public Library in December, which raised over $100,000. The balls, held at historic venues throughout the region, would become a highlight of the Society's social year going forward.

Moving into the new millennium was a transition period in Detroit's cultural community. Within a few months, primary leadership vacancies at the DIA, DSO, Wright, DHM, and Cranbrook Institute of Science were filled. The Historical Department, with the approval of Commissioner John Booth, hired new museums director and Hamtramck native Dennis Zembala, previously executive director of the Baltimore Museum of Industry that he helped found in 1981. Together with DHS President Kevin Broderick and DHS Executive Director Dick Strowger, things were looking up. According to the annual report for the year ending in June 2000, state funding came in at $1 million, philanthropy and earned income were up 26 percent, and available funds stood at $3.8 million.

Museum visitors were treated to the award-winning exhibition "30 Who Dared: Detroiters Who Made a Difference," a popular "Salute to Tiger Stadium," and a groundbreaking exhibit and programming called "When the Spirit Moves: African American Dance in History and Art," produced in partnership with the Wright Museum.

Significantly, the "Streets of Old Detroit" closed for its first major renovation since opening in 1951. Added were the 1900s dentist office, the Cadillac Café (today the Railroad Depot gallery), and interactive audiovisual components to the 1840s Schoolhouse. It reopened in January 2001. The Dossin Great Lakes Museum featured an exciting installation called "Frontier Metropolis," based on Brian Leigh Dunnigan's visually rich book of pre–photographic era images of the Detroit River region published by Wayne State University Press.

The education staff launched a new website that same month and partnered with Wayne County Regional Educational Service Agency and Detroit Public

Television on the show and video called *Motor City and You*. Behind the scenes, the Detroit Historical Museum received a $1.5 million interior environmental systems upgrade via City bonds.

The Historical Department and DHS were included in preparations for the commemoration of Cadillac's landing in 1701. *Detroit300*, under the direction of former Museum Director Maud Lyon, was a weeklong festival. As in 1951, the 2001 event included a costumed canoe landing, memorials, and fireworks. The grand dedication this time was for a new Riverfront Promenade. Even grander was the gathering of twenty-four historic tall ships and several days of nonstop music in Detroit's Hart Plaza and Dieppe Park in Windsor featuring dozens of Detroit's most iconic local and national performers.

In spring 2002, within only a few weeks, Robert "Bob" Bury, Tracy Smith (later Irwin), and Michelle VanOotegham (later Wooddell) joined the Detroit Historical Society staff. Each would play a significant role in the reinvention of the Society over the next nineteen years. Bury was hired as executive director and chief executive officer to succeed Dick Strowger, having served as an executive at SBC Ameritech (formerly Michigan Bell Telephone) and as development director at the Detroit Science Center. VanOotegham was brought in as fundraising director and soon became chief operating officer. Smith was initially tasked with addressing databases and public programming and later became chief exhibitions and enrichment officer.

The Historical Department launched a number of high-profile exhibits, including the critically acclaimed "Techno: Detroit's Gift to the World" and "Guts, Games and Glory: Detroit's Sporting Legacy," which opened in May 2003 and was a fan favorite that resulted in significant contributions to the collection.

At the Dossin, the Oliver Dewey Marcks Foundation funded the installation of an interpretive theater, designed to look like a freighter's cargo hold. The long-term exhibition "City on the Straits: History and Ecology of the Detroit River" was joined in 2002 by the innovative "Working the Inland Seas: Stories of African Americans on the Great Lakes," one of the first installations in the region to feature Black sailors.

The Education Department interacted with over 100,000 students through the Society's website, tours, and summer camp. The volunteer corps put in 16,000 hours and helped reopen portions of Historic Fort Wayne. Also, in 2002 the DHS programs team created the long-running Halloween feature, "Treats in the Streets," bringing hundreds of costumed children and their parents to the "Streets of Old Detroit."

While the fourth Society Ball, held at Marygrove College in 2002, brought in $150,000, the failure of "Arts, Parks, Kids" Proposal K at the ballot box and

Dave Wilborn, banjo player with the original McKinney's Cottonpickers, discusses the band's revival with Curator James Conway in 1974.

Juan Atkins spinning at the kickoff party for the 2003 Techno exhibition at the Detroit Historical Museum, held at the Roostertail nightclub.

significant budget cuts by city and state meant that the museums recorded a shortfall of $1.15 million as of June 30, 2003.

### CHANGING FORTUNES AT CITY HALL

Continued funding issues within the City of Detroit, stretching well beyond the Historical Department, prompted the administration of Mayor Kwame Kilpatrick to approach the Society, through the Detroit Historical Commission, about taking over management of the City's historical assets. Such an arrangement was seen as a way to keep the doors to these high-profile cultural assets open. A similar arrangement already existed with the DIA's Founders Society and was in the works for the Detroit Zoological Society. Under the arrangement, the City agreed to use its best efforts to provide annual funding of $500,000, ultimately saving the municipality about $1.5 million per year. Negotiations took place over many months and involved Bury, Broderick, and successor to the Society presidency, Francis W. "Sandy" McMillan II.

The Detroit Historical Society agreed to manage the Woodward Avenue museum, the Belle Isle museum, and the massive archive and artifact holdings in the Collections Resource Center at Historic Fort Wayne. The Society did not take responsibility for most of Fort Wayne, all monuments and statues previously overseen by the Historical Department, the Palmer Log Cabin, and the Moross House, which was later sold. The City retained ownership of all properties. Broderick reported that the mayor's office was highly supportive of the Society's initiative. During negotiations, there was even talk of bringing the Burton Historical Collection into the agreement and enlarging the Detroit Historical Museum facilities, neither of which came to fruition.

In mid-February, when the deal was imminent, the City laid off twelve employees and others departed for positions elsewhere in the government. Over the next few weeks, the Society staff of six and numerous volunteers kept the museums open. Bury's eleven-year-old daughter Meredith helped Dontez Bass (today the Society's longest-serving staffer) collect donations at the front desk; Michelle's father and Tracy did the same. Docents who were part of the Historical Department's education crew volunteered with the Society to assist with interpretation and visitors. The Glancy Trains ran on time.

On March 22, 2006, the Detroit City Council approved the Memorandum of Understanding between the City and the Society by a vote of 7–1, with one councilwoman absent. A few museum employees were retained for a short time during the transitions, but by the end of the year, the Detroit Historical Commission and Detroit Historical Department existed only on paper.

To say that the Society was unprepared for this would be unfair. Who could have prepared? Tracy Smith recalled, "There were keys everywhere, and papers everywhere. We were going through offices and drawers looking for contracts and plans, lighting schematics, and instructions for a DOS-based HVAC system." Bury remembered Dennis Bouchard, the Historical Department's helpful operations manager, sharing a desk drawer full of keys and sympathetically wishing him good luck. The museums stayed open.

Interaction with affinity groups and community partners went through an adjustment period. Behind the Scenes tours continued, and management of the retail business passed from the Detroit Historical Society Guild to the Society, while the Guild continued to raise money through the flea market and themed tea parties. The Society of the Colonial Dames, which designed the church tours, received facilitation assistance from the Society and after 2008 gradually transitioned completely; most revenues went to the venues. The Black Historic Sites Committee and Glancy Trains team simply began working directly with the Society. The Society and GLMI merged to form a new affinity group called the Maritime Auxiliary Group and later the Dossin Maritime Group. While several aspects of the blending worked well, particularly regarding special programming, it was dissolved in 2015. The organizations still work together on special programs and fundraising projects.

Overall, this new operating model necessitated the commitment of everyone, and efforts were made to reengage long-time board members, add new members, and establish several working committees to help guide Society leadership and staff as they faced what proved to be a monumental challenge.

The Society immediately undertook a "museum makeover" to freshen up some permanent exhibits and update temporary installations with new material. In some cases, these were fun replacements, like the "A to Z" exhibition of artifacts from the collection at the DHM, and "Maritime Marvels" at the Dossin museum. The following year, guest curator Janet Andersen stepped in to help produce "Building Boom: Detroit in the 1920s."

The Kresge Gallery's "Detroit's Fabulous 5" series of pop culture exhibits was introduced, along with preliminary versions of the "Detroit Artist Showcase," "New to the Collection," and "Motor City Showplace"—all long-time favorites. The Dossin museum highlighted yachting and boating "Clubs: A Shoreside Tradition" in DeRoy Hall, while "City on the Straits" and the pilothouse were refreshed.

Notably, 2007 saw the debut of the Community Gallery. This outreach initiative, spearheaded by Tracy Smith, allowed regional nonprofit organizations to tell their stories in Alger Hall for three-month periods. Guest organizations were responsible for design, content, and funding, while Society staff provided professional direction, installation, and technical support. This program drew attention within the national museum community, was presented at the AAM conference, and was later replicated elsewhere. Partnerships were also formed with traditional media outlets, raising the Society's profile, and incorporated the "Adventure Pass" program, which was linked to local libraries in southeast Michigan.

Programming became a focal point for marketing and outreach. The Behind the Scenes and Historic Houses of Worship tours were extremely popular but generated only modest revenue. In October 2006, the new Junior Benefit Committee, the Society's first young professional leadership group, worked with the programs staff to produce the hugely successful "Taste of the D," which brought local food purveyors and regional craft brewers into the "Streets of Old Detroit." African American Family Day, part of the monthlong celebration of Black History Month in February 2007, similarly brought in entertainment and craft vendors to fill the museum. The Dossin Gala and Society Ball generated $193,000, and the Society closed out this year of transition $414,000 in the black, with an even balance sheet.

The next few years saw gradual and steady growth of capability and staff. Despite a dramatic economic collapse that particularly affected Detroit, attendance for events, school tours, special tours, and facility rentals grew. New programs included an Author's Series, Curator Chats, Scholar's Series, and Film Series. A *Revolutionary Detroit* symposium in April 2009, and subsequent book publication, produced by Curator Joel Stone in partnership with Wayne State University's Department of History, was a scholarly success.

Thomas C. Buhl succeeded Sandy McMillan as Society board president in 2010 and served two four-year terms. Buhl was instrumental in leading the effort to secure funding and support for both major initiatives of this decade, through bad times and good. The Society Ball continued to draw attention to historic Detroit by hosting events at venues as diverse as the Fountain Ballroom at the Masonic Temple, Harley Earle's GM design studio in the Argonaut Building, and Shed 3 at historic Eastern Market. Each year the crowd grew, as did its generosity. By 2016, the Society Balls were generating $500,000, and the Dossin's "Spring into Belle Isle," $100,000.

In 2011, at the depth of the Great Recession and just as the City of Detroit was about to enter bankruptcy, Sandy McMillan, Tom Buhl, and Bob Bury publicly announced a $21.3 million comprehensive fundraising campaign. Dubbed *Past>Forward*, it had been underway for three years and was almost 70 percent pledged. The timing was perfect, as was the campaign leadership of past DHS President Kevin Broderick and trustees Ann Greenstone and David Nicholson.

The *Past>Forward* campaign was designed to allow the Society to reinvent about 75 percent of the museum and preen the other areas. While two-year development for all of the new *Past>Forward* exhibits was in process, exhibitions continued to change regularly at both museums, prior to the installation shutdown on May 24, 2012. "Detroit's Fabulous 5" topics included snack foods and great TV hosts—the members-only exhibit openings were known for being fun. Extended installations included wedding traditions and fashions, underwater archaeology, racing, and—a perennial favorite—toys. An online collections portal was launched that allowed anyone in the world to research digitized assets like photographs and ship plans, which were approaching 20,000 items. Tour programs expanded by 25 percent. The curatorial department produced another symposium and book, *Border Crossings: The Detroit River Region in the War of 1812*, a project that won Historical Society of Michigan and AASLH awards.

New web-based offerings included the "Encyclopedia of Detroit," as well as the online learning game "Building Detroit" for grades 3–5. The latter, championed by Director of Education Tobi Voigt (later chief curatorial officer) and funded by the Community Foundation of Southeast Michigan, garnered accolades from AAM and AASLH. The Education Department also reimagined the "Historical Perspectives" and "Maritime" tours aimed at school groups and hosted Michigan History Day. Despite the small staff size and budgetary limitations, the Society realized the *Past>Forward* vision.

On November 17, 2012, the Detroit Historical Museum reopened after six months with a black-tie gala event that drew 400 trustees and donors. On the twenty-third, the day after Thanksgiving, the museum opened to the public

Ivan Benning and his band perform in 2017 at "Jazz on the Streets of Old Detroit," a quarterly music series hosted by the Black Historic Sites Committee.

This 1966 Christmas Festival was similar to seasonal programs that filled Dodge Hall for over two decades.

Each year the Dossin Great Lakes Museum hosts the Lost Mariners Remembrance. Bagpiper Barbara Gator led the flagbearers in November 2012.

Family Day at the Detroit Historical Museum is part of programming for Black History Month in February, seen here in 2003.

Advertisement for the 150th Vernor's anniversary event in 2016.

1866 2016
150 YEARS
— VERNORS —

*Vernor's*

GINGER ALE

Celebrate the 150th anniversary of Vernors with a week of events!

June 5-11, 2016

detroithistorical.org
#Vernors150

with a free admission policy and stayed open for fifty-five straight hours, welcoming 15,000 visitors. Noel Night reportedly squeezed 12,000 people through in five hours! By the end of the fiscal year in June, membership was up 26 percent and retention solid. Retail sales netted $49,000, and volunteers logged 14,000 hours. Visitor surveys suggest that the temporary free-admission policy broadened the demographic make-up of the patrons. The policy went unaltered for several years.

New exhibits included the "Allesee Gallery of Culture" in Round Hall. The gift shop occupying that space moved to the Kresge Gallery, previously host to "Detroit's Fabulous 5." Stark Hall became an interactive music history experience named for entertainer and donor Kid Rock, and the "Motor City" exhibition was retooled as "America's Motor City." The gallery includes the "Automotive Showplace," a rotating vehicle highlight at the entrance, and "Automotive Showcase," a rotating topic-specific space at the opposite end of the gallery. The "Cadillac Body Drop," first installed in 1995, received a technological upgrade and remained the centerpiece.

The museum's second floor saw the addition of the "Gallery of Innovation," "Detroit: The Arsenal of Democracy," "Detroit Artist Showplace," and a vastly improved "Doorway to Freedom: Detroit and the Underground Railroad" in the former Tavy Stone Library space (much fashion material was relocated to Wayne State University's College of Design). The "Streets of Old Detroit," where for security reasons most shops had been closed to the public except during tours, was reopened with a few more elements of interpretation designed to not jar the period appeal that everyone remembers. The rest of the museum, including the auditorium and "Frontiers to Factories," got new LED lighting, fresh paint, and carpeting. A significant amount of the *Past>Forward* funds was spent addressing particular infrastructure needs, in partnership with the City, including ventilation and security system upgrades, as well as support for ongoing operations.

The Dossin Great Lakes Museum closed just before Christmas to undergo a similar grand renovation. A new gas HVAC system, funded through the recession-era American Recovery and Reinvestment Act of 2009, replaced the ancient electrical boiler system. The main gallery, host of the "City on the Straits" exhibit, became "Built by the River," telling the story of Detroit through the lens of its maritime history, from furs to industry to recreation. The S.S. *William Clay Ford* pilothouse received additional interpretation related to its part in the S.S. *Edmund Fitzgerald* search in 1975. DeRoy Hall lost its pageant of fleet flags but gained its stage centerpiece: the large oil painting of the Battle of Lake Erie that adorned the grand staircase of the S.S. *Greater Detroit* of the Detroit & Cleveland Navigation Company. LED lighting was installed throughout. The grand reopening took place on May 17, 2013, with a ticketed event for 400 guests, and opened to the public the following day.

Both *Past>Forward* museum renovations won AASLH awards, prompted huge boosts in attendance and facility rentals—the latter topping two hundred over twelve months—and gained the museum positive attention nationally. It should be noted that key partners in this process were Good Design Group, Morley Co., Wall Street Productions, and L. S. Brinker Co. They are all Michigan companies—a conscious decision during the Great Recession—and the results from these teams were so dynamic that the same players were retained for the Next Big Thing.

The Next Big Thing kicked off in 2014 and proved a game-changer for the organization—and arguably for the city's cultural community—and would absorb much of the Society's attention for the next five years. The Next Big Thing was addressing the 50th anniversary of the civil uprising that occurred in Detroit in 1967, generally called the "Riots" and later the "Rebellion."

This was an anniversary the Society had been anticipating for several years. While dozens of cities across the nation experienced similar uprisings in the 1960s, only Detroit and Newark, New Jersey, contemplated commemorations. Plans for such an exhibition were not well received in many quarters, but Society executives Bob Bury, Kate Baker, and Tobi Voigt convinced the Board of Trustees that this was a "go big or go home" moment for the organization. What had been envisioned as a temporary exhibition grew into a massive community engagement project, pulling in entities well beyond the Cultural Center.

Marlowe Stoudamire was hired as director for the project that became *Detroit67: Looking Back to Move Forward.* He helped Bury define the $4 million project and sell it to corporations and philanthropic foundations. Kalisha Davis was brought in to a newly created temporary position as the director of community outreach and engagement, initially funded by the Detroit Revitalization Fellows program.

From an engagement standpoint, by 2017 over 110 diverse organizations were on board, from the DIA to the Detroit Police Department to small neighborhood churches. The DHS website and social media served as a community calendar, and community partners participated in focus groups that helped define the entire project. One result was that the organization collected over 300 oral histories that gave the project its voice and served as a road map for the exhibition.

The broadly diverse nature of the project got the attention of major funding organizations, many of which had never supported the Society before. They made it possible to mount a $1 million, 3,000-square-foot exhibition, "Detroit 1967: Perspectives," which opened a month prior to the July 23 anniversary.

Round Hall as it appeared in 1953, serving as the museum entrance lobby. Later, the Old Detroit Shoppe occupied this space.

Round Hall became the "Allesee Gallery of Culture" during the *Past>Forward* campaign in 2012.

The open nature of the original Dodge Hall in 1954.

"America's Motor City" was updated during the *Past>Forward* campaign in 2012. The "Cadillac Body Drop" is seen to the right.

In terms of technology and temperament, it was like nothing the museum had ever offered the community and resulted in almost 200 successful programs like the "Design Detroit 2067" educational program and "Third Thursday" lecture and panel series; it also brought student and professional visitors from around the world. The overall "D67 project"—its internal nickname—and its book, *Detroit1967: Origins, Impacts, Legacies*, garnered nine awards, including the coveted National Medal from the Institute for Museum and Library Service and the History in Progress (HIP) Award from AASLH, and brought the Society second-place honors in the international "Best in Heritage: Projects with Influence" conference of the European Heritage Association.

Of course, as with the *Past>Forward* campaign, normal museum business was taking place at the same time as D67. Education staff expanded the internship program to a dozen students per year, created an "Arsenal of Democracy" teaching tool for high schoolers, and launched a Teacher's Portal designed with assistance from many regional curriculum experts. In an effort to expand accessibility, the Society became a founding member of the Michigan Alliance for Cultural Accessibility, and partnerships were formed with the Alzheimer's Association-Greater Michigan Chapter and KultureCity to improve accommodations for guests with sensory needs.

The exhibitions and curatorial staff developed some fun and classy installations, including "Out on the Town: Drinking and Dining in Detroit since 1920," "Fashion D:Fined: The Past, Present and Future of Detroit Fashion," and wonderful counterculture features on poster artist Gary Grimshaw and Detroit's 1960s-era radical press. Photography was prominent, with "Heart and Soul Detroit" showing famous Detroiters through the lens of photographer Jenny Risher, and "Motown Black & White" spotlighting the famous music company through photographs from promotional guru Al Abrams's collection. Additionally, the Society secured a Knights Arts Challenge grant to revisit legendary Detroit photographer Bill Rauhauser's 1970–1980s "Documenting Detroit" student project at the College for Creative Studies, creating "Redocumenting Detroit."

The Dossin museum hosted the science-based exhibitions "Troubled Waters: Healing Our Freshwater Habitats" and "How Does That Work?" as well as "Guardians of the Great Lakes" about government mariners.

The online archival collection topped 40,000 images by 2015, and attention was turned to film and video assets, including a collection of over 5,000 items received from the City of Detroit's Communications Department in 2015. These soon became the core of a revenue stream not previously available. Work was also completed on scanning and cataloging material related to the U.S. Lake Survey Office, Packard Motors, Parke-Davis Pharmaceuticals, Detroit River ferries, Bob-Lo boats, and Gregory Boat Company, as well as a priceless hydro-

Previously, the Robert E. Lee gallery hosted models and rotating exhibitions, as seen in this 1960 photograph.

At the Dossin Great Lakes Museum, the renamed John A. and Marlene L. Boll Foundation Gallery was updated with "Built by the River" in 2013.

plane photograph collection. In addition to digitization, conservation was completed on a cannon barrel recovered from the river in 2011—it was placed on display at the Dossin—and a full inventory of the Collections Resource Center was launched, resulting in a better understanding of the true nature of its holdings and creating new accessions for well over 4,000 orphaned items.

Public relations and marketing, under the direction of Chief Development and Communications Officer Rebecca Salminen-Witt and Marketing & Public Relations Manager Sarah Murphy, helped bring the Society further into the social media world; its first mention in annual reports comes in 2016. High on the list of successes was the Vernor's 150th Anniversary Party, celebrating a revered local ginger ale. On June 11, 2016, in addition to a Vernor's pop-up exhibit and daylong series of programming that included a citywide scavenger hunt, over 2,000 people set the record for "most people drinking Vernor's at the same time." The Facebook feed hit 850,000 views with no advanced buzz . . . or fizz.

Visitorship was approaching 150,000 at all facilities and events. Membership grew 400 percent in a few years to over 2,300, largely through continued free admission and D67 partnerships. Retail sales were reported as $154,000 at DHM and $22,600 at Dossin in 2015. Facility rentals continued to grow. The DHM got a new roof, a new parking lot, and two new trucks. The Dossin had new gas lines and high-speed digital connections installed by the City.

Approaching the new decade, the Detroit Historical Society was savoring the success of the D67 project and looking at the *next* Next Big Thing, which turned out to be multiple "things." On the radar, of course, was anticipation of the organization's 100th anniversary in late 2021. Looming equally large was the announced departure of Bob Bury as Society executive director and CEO, and passing of the gavel on the Board of Trustees from Tom Buhl to John Decker.

In June 2018, the Board of Trustees announced that Elana Rugh would succeed Bob Bury. Elana brought many years of experience in the nonprofit sector in Detroit as president of the Michigan Chapter of the National Multiple Sclerosis Society and as a development executive at Henry Ford Health System and Detroit Country Day School. Trustee John Decker, a partner at the law firm Jaffe Raitt Heuer and Weiss since 2003, had been an invaluable advisor to the Society as chair of the Governance Committee.

Initiatives set in motion prior to this transition would maintain momentum, including a fresh fundraising campaign to reimagine the landscaping at the Belle Isle campus, initiated and visioned by then COO Kate Baker. With backing from the Dossin family and a handful of private donors, new exterior elements would enhance the site's versatility and access, whether arriving by car or kayak to peruse or party. Equally in play was the City's future use of

Visitors to the "Motor City Music" exhibition stop at the tribute to Aretha Franklin following her death in 2018.

A Muslim wedding dress was part of "Saying I Do" in 2010 that explored sixteen ethnic wedding traditions in Detroit.

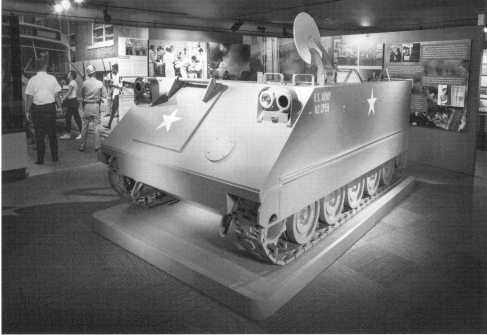

The prototype Mustang II is featured in the rotating "Motor City Showplace" display at the entrance to "America's Motor City" in 2012.

This armored personnel carrier replica, a featured display in the "Detroit67: Perspectives" exhibition of 2017, also served as a mid-gallery theater.

Historic Fort Wayne in response to the new Gordie Howe International Bridge being constructed adjacent to the fort, perhaps affecting both the collection's condition and future location.

Change comes naturally with any transition of leadership. Following her arrival, Rugh endeavored to understand and respect the experiences and opinions of the staff, board, volunteers, and visitors. Perpetuating internal changes sparked by the D67 project was a priority, particularly those related to employee culture, diversification of the staff, and a commitment to increasing equity, accessibility, and inclusion throughout the visitor experience.

Reinforcing that commitment, the Woodward museum hosted the photograph exhibition "Invisible No Longer: LGBTQ+ Detroit," focused on Detroit's reaction to the 50th anniversary of New York's Stonewall Riots in 1969. Later, a nostalgic reimagining of the Lindell AC sports bar was installed in Wrigley Hall on the lower level of the museum. Free music returned to the BankOne Plaza with "Lunchtime Techno" in summer 2019 and fall 2020. And after a dozen successful years, the newly renamed Robert and Mary Ann Bury Community Gallery program garnered the 2019 AASLH Leadership in History Award for its innovative longevity.

The no-fee admission policy, which was introduced as a short-term experiment in 2012 and extended to promote inclusivity, proved financially unsustainable. New membership levels were created, with a complimentary category available to residents of Detroit, Highland Park, and Hamtramck. Because all other venues on Belle Isle were admission-free, the Dossin Great Lakes Museum remained open-access but enjoyed impressive showings at the donation box.

On the business side, the development team created "The Course of History Golf Classic." Launched in 2019, this annual celebrity fundraiser has been held on historic courses at the Detroit Golf Club and the Country Club of Detroit. As the Society approached its centennial, the Finance Department did an extensive redesign of administrative policies and procedures including migrating to a state-of-the-art donor, patron, and visitor tracking platform. Marketing and public relations staff continue to spread the word that "Detroit Starts Here" and that the Detroit Historical Society is committed to making the museums accessible and engaging for everyone. Helping with that challenge, the DHS volunteer corps—a diverse and invaluable part of the Society family—had grown to over 150 by spring 2020.

## A GLOBAL STUMBLE

In early March 2020, employees were being advised to work from home due to the aggressive worldwide spread of a novel coronavirus for which there was no available vaccine. Operations staff quickly facilitated work-at-home tools for the staff, and on March 13 the museums were closed due to COVID-19 and remained so until July 10. The isolation tactics were generally successful, and while most staff remained healthy, the pandemic took a heavy toll on extended family and friends. A stunning blow came when community leader and former D67 Project Director Marlowe Stoudamire died of the virus. Former DHS Executive Director Michael W. R. Davis also succumbed.

In this unknown climate, the staff leveraged their strengths. The leadership team, in cooperation with Midtown Detroit, Inc., and NSF International, worked to define safe reopening protocols and identify resources to implement them. The finance team secured federal funds to retain most staff through the shutdown. All other departments began promoting and augmenting the Society's existing online resources, understanding that, at least for the near future, virtual programs were the only avenue for visitor interaction.

Fortunately, digital resources for the most immediate community needs were already accessible: teacher lesson plans, student research material, and primary documents. Helpful tips for preserving family photos and heirlooms during a "stay-at-home" period were also available. Indeed, global sales for digital assets, particularly films and photographs, kept the collections staff busy and generated much-needed revenue.

In creative ways, the Society's social calendar went digital. The annual gala on Belle Isle became "Toast to the Dossin," and the 99th Annual Meeting was digitally enabled for the Society's forty-five trustees and other members. In January 2021, the Boom Town Ball fundraiser entertained 192 patrons and guests in their homes with a virtual preview of the recently opened exhibit "Boom Town: Detroit in the 1920s" as a nod to the Society's centennial. The event, which included doorstep delivery of gourmet meals and wine, raised more than $150,000. Among the few in-person events, and to everyone's delight, dedication of the outdoor enhancements at the Dossin Great Lakes Museum was held on August 29. The Lost Mariners Remembrance in November was a hybrid, with a live lantern and wreath ceremony and prerecorded musical and historical presentations.

The education team touted fresh virtual tours of core exhibitions, and the community outreach team launched entertaining and award-winning "Detroit History Heroes" and "Pint-Sized Prohibition," a short-form video series including outreach. October 2020's "Detroit's Brewing Heritage" exhibit opening was accompanied by a live "Beer Trail" tour, a presentation slot at the 2020 Beer Culture Summit in Chicago, and a special podcast series. The beer turned to whiskey for a "Bourbon and Bowties" bourbon trail in the spring. Speakers Bureau presentations were available via live streaming or prerecorded selections.

The Society helped the Detroit Symphony celebrate Orchestra Hall's centenary in 2019 with this Robert and Mary Ann Bury Community Gallery installation, as well as installations at the Max M. and Marjorie S. Fisher Music Center.

The WGPR William V. Banks Broadcast Museum & Media Center partnered with the Black Historic Sites Committee to produce this Community Gallery exhibit in 2016.

A century of amateur theater was the focus of this Community Gallery focused on the Player's Playhouse in 2018.

The Oral History Project, which had repositioned itself to capture voices of Detroit's neighborhoods, pivoted to cover the devastation of the pandemic and the almost simultaneous civil uprisings in the spring and summer of 2020, which cast the D67 project in a renewed light. The Community Gallery sported a celebration of Orchestra Hall's 100th Anniversary followed by "2000/2020: Celebrating 20 Years of the Electronic Music Festival in Detroit," which also became a virtual exhibition in January 2021. Relationships with the Great Lakes Maritime Institute, the Black Historic Sites Committee, and the Glancy Trains volunteers remained as strong as ever.

## LOOKING FORWARD

There are intriguing things in the Society's future. Internally, a fresh urgency is driving strategic development of engaging digital education resources and outreach tools. Existing online materials, such as the "Encyclopedia of Detroit," are constantly reviewed for accuracy and balance, similar to long-term physical exhibitions and programming options. Facility upgrades required for the collection and galleries are pending.

Externally, there are also plans to transform the city's 83-acre Midtown cultural area into a cohesive district characterized by walkable public space connecting twelve cultural institutions. Called "Detroit Square," the goal is to create a signature destination for visitors and residents alike. The Detroit Historical Museum sits at the northwest boundary of Detroit Square, and dynamic activation of this corner will create a new prominence for the Detroit Historical Museum as the gateway to the district.

To take full advantage of the plans for Detroit Square, the Society endeavors to reopen the Woodward Avenue entrance and significantly redesign the museum's interior spaces to allow more flexibility in its exhibits and storytelling, ultimately leading to expanded community utilization, a richer visitor experience, and increased sustainability.

This is exciting. It is also a leap of faith. The Detroit Historical Society has made leaps of faith for a century—like starting yet another cultural club in a city full of clubs and putting a museum in a skyscraper. This organization will make such leaps again.

# APPENDIX A

## LIST OF PAST PRESIDENTS AND LEADERS
### (IN ORDER OF SERVICE)

PRESIDENTS OF THE BOARD OF TRUSTEES

Clarence Burton

Thomas A. E. Weadock

Orla B. Taylor

J. Bell Moran

George W. Stark

Dr. Alfred H. Whittaker

J. Bell Moran

Reuben Ryding

Prentiss Brown

Harold M. Hastings

Hazel (Mrs. Wilson W.) Mills

Marquis F. Shattuck

Ben R. March

Gordon O. Rice

Paul L. Penfield

Ruth (Mrs. Leland W.) Foster

H. Richard Steding III

Mark C. Stevens

Walter J. Murray

William S. Schindler

Barbara (Mrs. R. Alexander)
    Wrigley

Hudson Mead

Henry Earle

Donald Lindow

Alan L. Gormick

Warren J. Wilkinson

Philip G. Moon

John L. Booth II

Susan (Mrs. William P.) Vititoe

Mary Lou (Mrs. Morton) Zieve

Kevin Broderick

Francis W. "Sandy" McMillan II

Thomas Buhl

John Decker

SOCIETY EXECUTIVE DIRECTORS

Nancy D. Cunningham

John Buckbee

Michael W. R. Davis

Bill Zoufal

Lynne Aldrich

Dick Strowger

Bob Bury

Elana Rugh

MUSEUM DIRECTORS (*ITALICS INDICATES
CITY OF DETROIT HISTORICAL DEPARTMENT*)

| | |
|---|---|
| Arthur Hampton (caretaker/curator) | 1928–1943 |
| Robert Larson | 1943–1946 |
| *Raymond Miller* | *1946–1947* |
| *Henry Brown* | *1947–1970* * |
| *Solon Weeks* | *1970–1984* |
| *Betty J. Allen* | *1984–1985 (acting)* |
| *Barry Dressel* | *1985–1990* |
| *Maud Lyon* | *1990–1999* |
| *Vicky Kruckeberg* | *1999–2000 (interim)* |
| *Dennis Zembala* | *2000–2006* |
| Bob Bury | 2006–2018 |
| Elana Rugh | 2018– |

DETROIT HISTORICAL COMMISSION PRESIDENTS/CHAIRPERSONS

George Stark
Leonard N. Simons
Charles V. Hagler
Barbara (Mrs. R. Alexander) Wrigley
Warren J. Wilkinson
John L. Booth II

* *From 1954 to 1966, George Stark was president of the Historical Commission and managing director of the Historical Department. Henry Brown was simultaneously museums director for the Historical Department and coordinating director, an ex-officio member of the Society board.*

# APPENDIX B

## DETROIT HISTORICAL SOCIETY BALL LOCATIONS

| | |
|---|---|
| 1999 | Detroit Public Library |
| 2000 | Guardian Bldg. |
| 2001 | Masonic Temple |
| 2002 | Marygrove College—Madame Cadillac Hall |
| 2003 | Fisher Bldg. |
| 2004 | City Airport |
| 2005 | Detroit Yacht Club |
| 2006 | Stroh Riverplace |
| 2007 | Roostertail |
| 2008 | Weston-Book Cadillac |
| 2009 | Dearborn Inn |
| 2010 | Argonaut Building—Design Studio |
| 2011 | Eastern Market—Shed 3 |
| 2012 | Detroit Historical Museum |
| 2013 | Fillmore Theater |
| 2014 | Masonic Temple—Fountain Ballroom |
| 2015 | Packard Plant |
| 2016 | Joe Louis Arena |
| 2017 | Corktown Factory |
| 2018 | Lexus Velodrome |
| 2020 | State Savings Bank Building* |
| 2021 | Boom Town Virtual Ball |

*Note: The Society's long-running Christmas Pageant gradually grew into a holiday open house and starting in 1981 a fundraiser called the Historical Society Gala. Most took place at the Detroit Historical Museum. In 1988 it was held at the newly renovated Wayne County Building. In 1999, the Detroit Historical Society Ball began rotating among historically significant venues in the city.*

\* Ball moved from December to January.

# APPENDIX C

## CASS LECTURESHIP SERIES

1948   Stanley M. Pargellis, "Father Gabriel Richard"

1950   Raymond Miller, "The Importance of Being Earnest"

1951   Frank B. Woodford, "Yankees in Wonderland"

1952   R. Darwin Burroughs, "Exploration Unlimited"

1953   S. K. Stevens, "Local History Is Living History"

1954   Milo M. Quaife, "The Yankees Capture York"

1955   Prentiss M. Brown, "The Mackinac Bridge Story"

1956   Albert B. Corey, "Canadian-American Relations along the Detroit River"

1957   Avery O. Crave, "A Frontier Cycle"

1958   Edward P. Alexander, "The Museum: A Living Book of History"

1959   Bruce Catton, "Michigan's Past and the Nation's Future"

1960   R. Carlyle Buley, "The Romantic Appeal of the New West—1815–1840"

1961   Arthur Pound, "The Automobile and an American City"

1962   Harlan H. Hatcher, "Revolutions of Aspiration"

1963   Howard H. Peckham, "Life in Detroit under Pontiac's Siege"

1964   Walter Havighurst, "The Shadowed Name of Henry Hamilton, Governor of Detroit, 1775–1779"

1965   Roscoe O. Bonisteel, "John Monteith, Man of Conscience"

1966   Francis Paul Prucha, "Lewis Cass and American Indian Policy"

1967   James Parton, "The Legacy of Neglect"

1968   James J. Kilpatrick, "The Topless Bathing Suit and Other Footnotes to American History"

1969   Robert S. Byrd, "The Decline—But Not Yet the Fall—of the Russian Empire"

# APPENDIX D

## HISTORY OF MAJOR SUPPORT GROUPS

### ALGONQUIN CLUB OF DETROIT AND WINDSOR

The club was founded on March 27, 1934, by Dr. Milo M. Quaife, a teacher and scholar of regional history. Dr. Quaife, while secretary and editor of the Burton Historical Collection, conducted seminars focused on the history of the Old Northwest at the University of Detroit (today University of Detroit-Mercy) and Wayne University (today Wayne State University). The club also provided sponsorship for regional history events, such as the Historical Society of Michigan's annual Local History Conference.

Historians-without-borders, for many decades the primary feature of the Algonquin Club was monthly membership meetings held alternately in Detroit and Windsor, featuring a dinner and historical presentation. They also published a monthly newsletter called *The Algonquin*. The Algonquin Club name was chosen by the club's early members "to perpetuate the memory of the family of Indian tribes that originally inhabited this area." Due to declining membership, the club suspended its regular meeting schedule in September 2019.

### BLACK HISTORIC SITES COMMITTEE

The Black Historic Sites Committee (BHSC) was formed in 1971 in response to a suggestion by former Detroit City Councilman Ernest C. Browne Jr. The committee is devoted to educating the public about the significant contributions African Americans have made to the history of Detroit. The BHSC was created with a diverse membership and continues in that tradition today.

As an affinity group of the Detroit Historical Society, the BHSC works with the Society to develop and implement a variety of services, programs, and activities that include creating exhibits, tours, activities, special events, publications, and educational materials to stimulate interest in Detroit's African American community.

Since its inception, the Black Historic Sites Committee has guided placement of over a dozen Michigan Historical Markers. Most recently the BHSC led an effort to have the Detroit Plaindealer Historical Marker installed in downtown Detroit. The paper, founded in 1883, was Detroit's first Black-owned newspaper. Plans are underway to have the newly approved Michigan Historical Marker for Black Bottom neighborhood installed at Lafayette Park. The Black Historic Sites Bus Tours program, relaunched in 2018, takes passengers to sites with Michigan Historical Markers dedicated to African Americans.

Over the years the Black Historic Sites Committee has entertained the public through a variety of programs. The popular "Jazz on the Streets of Old Detroit" celebrates America's original art form with performances by its musical creators. In the area of sports history, the BHSC worked with DHS staff on an exhibit commemorating the 100th anniversary of the Detroit Stars, a Negro National League team. In 2020 the committee partnered with the Friends of Hamtramck Stadium to commemorate the 100th anniversary of the Negro League's founding with a panel of baseball historians.

In 2021 the BHSC celebrated its fifty-year anniversary of welcoming members with a passion for bringing Michigan's African American history to light.

## DAUGHTERS OF THE AMERICAN REVOLUTION IN MICHIGAN

The Daughters of the American Revolution (DAR) was founded in 1890 as a volunteer women's service organization dedicated to promoting patriotism, preserving American history, and securing America's future through better education for children. Today the national organization boasts 165,000 members in 3,000 chapters across the United States and internationally.

The first chapter in Michigan was the Louisa St. Clair Chapter in Detroit, today registered in Grosse Pointe. Organized in January 1893, it was the thirtieth chapter in the national society. Today, there are fourteen chapters in the metro Detroit area, all part of the DAR of Michigan, founded in 1900, which has approximately 3,000 women members.

From its inception the DAR has provided opportunities to cherish American heritage, preserve local histories, promote national holidays, and support our national defense.

## DETROIT HISTORICAL SOCIETY GUILD

This auxiliary group of the Detroit Historical Society grew out of the original Women's Committee of the Board of Trustees, formed in 1936. The Guild gained a public profile in 1951 with the opening of the Detroit Historical

Museum and over the next fifty years would support numerous initiatives of the Society.

Initial Guild activities included organizing the Patriot's Balls at either the museum or a fancy hotel ballroom. It also sponsored educational teas for young ladies and historic fashion shows featuring costumes from the growing collection, and served as hostesses at the many receptions and events held at the museums each year. Christmas decorating in the "Streets of Old Detroit" was another Guild contribution.

Monetary support from the Detroit Historical Society Guild underwrote educational films, historical publications, and supplies for decades of school tours. Fundraising was accomplished with the balls and teas, as well as by managing the Old Detroit Shop at the Woodward museum, and through the "Attic Sales" (today "Flea Markets") at Historic Fort Wayne. Members gradually passed these latter duties to the DHS and the Historic Fort Wayne Coalition.

### GLANCY TRAINS BOARD AND MODULAR GROUP

One of Detroit's notable model train aficionados was Alfred R. Glancy Jr., a banking and real estate executive. Over many years he gathered rare and valuable model trains into an impressive private collection, running them on a grand railroad layout in his Grosse Pointe home. Upon his death in 1973, his heirs donated his beloved trains to the Detroit Historical Society.

Since then, a dedicated procession of hobbyists and volunteers have continued to build on Glancy's vision. Today, the updated model layout in the Detroit Historical Museum's lower level remains one of the most popular installations. Additionally, a second team of enthusiasts maintains the Glancy modular layout, a traveling exhibition that captivates young and old at festivals and other historical facilities in the region, such as Greenfield Village.

Together the museum and modular teams keep what was once one of America's favorite hobbies alive and engaging throughout the region, representing another jewel at the Detroit Historical Society.

### GREAT LAKES MARITIME INSTITUTE

As Detroit's Museum of Great Lakes History was becoming a reality following World War II, the focus of interpretation was on creating a series of accurate ship models, resulting in the Great Lakes Model Shipbuilders Guild. This group made or solicited dozens of extremely high-quality artworks illustrating changes in vessel design from canoes to massive steamers, all in the same 1/8 scale.

In 1960, as the Dossin Great Lakes Museum was built to replace the schooner *J. T. Wing*, the Guild became the Great Lakes Maritime Institute (GLMI) and broadened its mission to include physical and financial support for the museum. Visible evidence of its support includes many of the artifacts in the Society's collection, as well as major infrastructural investments in the S.S. *Edmund Fitzgerald* anchor recovery, *William Clay Ford* pilothouse, and—believe it or not—the parking lot.

GLMI has published *Telescope* magazine, containing historic and contemporary shipping news, since 1952. Since 1980, Captain Kathy McGraw—a former Dossin employee—has been the editor, with "Seaway News" led by Gregg Rudnick and many, many volunteer writers and researchers.

The organization helped recover the anchor of the S.S. *Greater Detroit* in 2017 and has led the powerful Lost Mariners Remembrance program each year on Belle Isle since 1995.

## HISTORIC MEMORIALS SOCIETY

The Historic Memorials Society in Detroit (HMSD) was originally founded in 1891 as the Mount Vernon Society of Detroit, a local unit of the Mount Vernon Ladies Association of the Union (the oldest women's charity organization in the United States). In 1922, the organization was renamed the Historic Memorials Society in Detroit and began its current mission of focusing on the preservation of civic memorials around the country and particularly the Detroit area.

Since its reorganization, the HMSD donated to more than 100 different organizations, funds, societies, and projects around the Detroit area and the state of Michigan and in several locations around the United States. The DHS was fortunate to be among those benefactors, with donations serving both programming and artifact acquisition. Due to declining membership, the organization suspended activities in 2014.

## INTERNATIONAL SHIPMASTERS ASSOCIATION— DETROIT LODGE #7

This fraternal organization was formed in 1886 by captains of commercial Great Lakes vessels as a mutual insurance association and to advocate for navigational improvements and safe working conditions. Today it represents all licensed mariners and supports efforts to preserve their industry's historical legacy.

The Detroit Lodge #7 became a member of ISMA in 1891 and today is the largest of the organization's lodges. From 1986 until 2006, Lodge #7 held its weekly meetings at the Dossin Great Lakes Museum and was instrumental in providing funding and technical expertise for the most significant additions and acquisitions during that period.

The Shipmasters still support the museum and, along with the Great Lakes Maritime Institute, are involved in projects to enhance the region's maritime history.

## MARINE HISTORICAL SOCIETY OF DETROIT

Born of a conversation at the Detroit Historical Museum high atop the Barlum Tower in 1943, the Marine Historical Society of Detroit (MHSD) held its first meeting there on July 13, 1944. By the end of the year, it was fully incorporated, driven by maritime enthusiasts Roy Bates, John O'Brien, Bob Larson, Bill McDonald, Norbert Neff, Ken Smith, Captain W. Taylor, and Alistair Weir—the listed founders. Significantly, Bates and Larson were trustees of the Detroit Historical Society.

Since then, the MHSD has been integral to chronicling the Great Lakes commercial shipping industry. The *Detroit Marine Historian*, published since 1947, is an invaluable resource for information about vessels, ports, companies, and characters of the freshwater seas.

## NATIONAL SOCIETY OF THE COLONIAL DAMES OF AMERICA IN THE STATE OF MICHIGAN

Founded in 1891, the National Society of the Colonial Dames of America (NSCDA) is a leader in today's preservation and interpretation of historic sites, traditions, and events. Headquartered in Dumbarton House in Washington, D.C., it sponsors preservation and patriotic projects, educational programs, and history scholarships to promote contemporary awareness of the national legacy.

The National Society of the Colonial Dames of America in the State of Michigan (NSCDA-MI) is one of forty-four national chapters and encourages programs and collaborations that stimulate interest in regional heritage. Members have supported historically significant projects for many years, not only with the Detroit Historical Museum and Historic Fort Wayne, where they were directly involved in the Commander's House project, but also at local universities and the Detroit Institute of Arts. The Dames recently helped fund restoration of the Sibley House at Christ Church Detroit and provided sponsorship for a Michigan War of 1812 Bicentennial Commission seminar.

# ACKNOWLEDGMENTS

THE Detroit Historical Society thanks the generations of people who made this book both necessary and possible. Special thanks to: Miss Gracie Krum, Mr. James Conway, and Mr. Robert Cosgrove for their work in chronicling the history of both the Society and the Detroit Historical Department; the secretaries, editors, and writers who contributed to a century of Society publications, which proved invaluable in this project; former executives and employees of the City and Society who provided interviews and reviewed pertinent portions of the text for correctness, including Bob Bury, Kevin Broderick, Dick Strowger, Maud Lyon, Jim Conway, Patience Nauta, and Cynthia Young; current employees who looked over the manuscript, helped polish it, and kept me honest, including Elana, Tracy, Rebecca, Malika, Casie, Gail, and Bree; Annie Martin and the team at Wayne State University Press who embraced this project from the start; and Douglas D. Fisher, who has edited four Society publications with the author, this one after a tough year. Thanks, Doug.

Heartfelt thanks to all prior and current educators, collections managers, curators, registrars, interns, and volunteers who have cared for Detroit's written and material history. Sometimes that one little piece of paper makes a big difference. Equal gratitude to the executives, docents, accountants, exhibit specialists, development pros, designers, building specialists, publicists, program and event managers, and visitor experience associates who have made these havens-of-history possible. Only through your efforts do the stories and artifacts reach a larger audience.

Volunteers deserve great thanks, starting with the Board of Trustees and the reliable corps of event, tour, docent, research, and collections assistants who have donated their time to our cause. Over a century, the number of donated hours is incalculable.

Besides our internal volunteers, the Society has been supported by innumerable fraternal, social, and business organizations. Knowing the hazards inherent in such lists, long-time friends and volunteer groups deserve to be mentioned. Omissions are the fault of the author.

Algonquin Club of Detroit and
    Windsor*
Association for the Study of Negro
    (today African American) Life
    and History
Black Historic Sites Committee*
Business Founders of Detroit
Daughters of the American Revolu-
    tion in Michigan*
Daughters of the War of 1812
Detroit Historical Society Guild*
Glancy Trains Board and Modular
    Group*
Goodfellows/Old Newsboys
Great Lakes Maritime Institute*

Historic Fort Wayne Coalition
Historic Memorials Society*
International Shipmasters Associa-
    tion—Detroit Lodge #7*
Kiwanis Club #1 Detroit
Marine Historical Society of
    Detroit*
National Society of the Colonial
    Dames of America in the State
    of Michigan*
Pioneers of Powerboating
Prismatic Club of Detroit
Propeller Club of Detroit
Sons of the War of 1812

*Short history in appendix D.*

# INDEX

Page numbers in *italics* refer to images.

accessibility, 113, 118

Alger, Russell A., 42

Algonquin Club, 57, 127

Allen, Betty, 79, 81

American Association for State and Local History (AASLH), 37, 57, 65, 106, 110, 113, 118

American Association of Museums (AAM), 37–38, 57, 105, 106

Andersen, Janet, 104

Annual Meetings, 28, 32, 33–34, 36, 38, 42, 44, 47–48, 57–59, 119

archival collection, 33, 47, 113–15

"Arts, Parks, Kids" Proposal K, 101

Atkins, Juan, *102*

auto centennial, 92–93

automobile manufacturing, 24, 76

Babcock, Myrtle, 33

Baker, Kate, 110, 115

Bald, F. Clever, 37, 59

Barlum Tower, 31–32, 33, 37–38, 43

Bass, Dontez, 103

Beck, Mary, 62, *63*

Beltaire, Mark, 61

Black Historic Sites Committee (BHSC), 74, 80, 104, *106*, *120*, 121, 127–28

Bob-Lo, 92, 113

Boom Town Ball, 119

Booth, John II, *69*, 84, 91, 96, 100

Booth-Wilkinson Costume Gallery, 83–84

Bouchard, Dennis, 104

Boyes, Edwin, 75

Breck, Peggy, *89*, 90

Broderick, Kevin, *69*, 85, 100, 103, 105

Brown, Henry, 22, 43, 47, 50, 51, *52*, 55, 57, 65, *66*, *67*, *68*, 72, 75

Brown, McPherson, 43

Brown, Prentiss, 48, 66

Brown, Sadie, *87*

Browne, Ernest C. Jr., 74, 127

Buhl, Thomas C. "Tom," *70*, 105, 115

Building Endowment Fund Committee, 43, 44

Burr, Karen, *86*, 87

Burton, Clarence, 19, 27, 31, 33, 35

Burton, Jack, 54

Burton, M. Agnes, 33, 34, 35, 60

Bury, Mary Ann, *70*, 118, 120

Bury, Meredith, 103

Bury, Robert "Bob," *70*, 99, 101, 104, 105, 110, 115, 118, 120

Butler, Louisa, 39, 43

Byrne, Robert, 80

*Cadillac's Homeland*, 65

Caito, Frank, 54

calendar, as fundraiser, 34, 100

Cass Lectures, 56–57, 126

Catlin, George, 27, 33

Cavanagh, Jerome, 65, *67*

Charles H. Wright Museum of African American History, 71–72, 96

Charter Amendment, 47

Children's Book Fair, 59, *85*

Christmas Open House, 59, 65, 73, *107*

civil rights movement, 71–72

Clark, Carl L., 60

Clark, Thomas E., 25, 59, 75

Cody, Frank, 43

Coletta, Paul, *88*
Collections Resource Center, 82, 85, 94, 115
community support organizations, 26
concrete, 25
Conference of Historical Societies, 37
Conway, Jim, 81, *102*
Cosgrove, Bob, 93
"Course of History Golf Classic, The," 118
COVID-19 pandemic, 118–21
Cunningham, Nancy, 80

Daughters of the American Revolution (DAR), 34, 72, 128
Davis, Kalisha, 110–13
Davis, Michael W. R., 96, 119
Decker, John, 115
Delaney, Sakunah, *86*, 87
DeRoy, Helen, 62–64, 66, 78
Detroit
  books on, 59
  riots in, 71, 110
  at turn of century, 22–26
*Detroit300*, 101
*Detroit67: Looking Back to Move Forward*, 110, 115, *117*, 118, 121
Detroit Arts Commission, 36
Detroit Business Pioneers, 35
Detroit Historical Commission, 22, 46–47, 48–50, 65–66, 83
Detroit Historical Department, 22, 54–56, 81, 83, 91, 101
Detroit Historical Museum
  in Barlum Tower, 31–33
  and civil rights movement, 71–72
  data entry and inventory processing at, 94–95
  exhibition design changes, 59–60
  exhibitions at Woodward museum, 56, 58, 80, 95–96
  exhibitions in 1990s, 95–96
  exhibitions in 2000s, 109, 113
  financial crisis's impact on, 99–100
  financial shortfalls of, 65
  fundraising for, 91
  increased membership and visitorship, 80, 115, 118

  opening of new, 50–54
  reopening of, 106–9
  and Replica Project, 36–37
  second phase of, 64–65, 71, 72
  shuttering of, 78, 79
  updates to, 104–5
  in Williams House, 46
Detroit Historical Society
  context of establishment of, 26
  cooperation between Historical Commission and Historical Department and, 83
  donations to, 29, 59, 79
  early years of, 27–39
  establishment of, 27–28
  expansion of Board of Trustees, 48
  fiftieth anniversary of, 75
  financial crisis's impact on, 99–100
  financial difficulties of, 79, 103
  funding for, 77, 81, 91, 96, 100, 105–6
  future of, 121–22
  during Great Depression, 35–37
  growth of, 21–22
  major support groups, 127–31
  membership events, 57–59
  membership levels and growth of, 31, 43, 80, 109, 115
  Memorandum of Understanding with Detroit, 103–4
  mission of, 19
  new building for, 42–44, 46
  outreach efforts of, 57
  past presidents and leaders of, 123–24
  preservation efforts of, 37, 48, 77, 115
  publications, 28, 44, 75, 105, 106, 113
  public relations and marketing for, 115
  records of, 20
  trustees of, 13, *66*
  women's early involvement in, 33–35
  youth program of, 38, 113
Detroit Historical Society Ball, 100, 105, 125
*Detroit Historical Society Bulletin*, 44–46, 49, 50–51, 65, 71, 75, 76
Detroit Historical Society Guild, 65, 72, 77, 81, 84, 104, 128–29
*Detroit in Perspective: A Journal of Regional History*, 75–76, 77

Detroit Institute of Arts, 42, 47, 91
Detroit Lodge #7, 130–31
Detroit Public Library (DPL), 19, 38
Detroit Square, 121–22
Dodge Hall, 91–92
donations, 29
Dossin, Robert, 62, *63*
Dossin, Roy, *67*
Dossin Dive Team, 90
Dossin Great Lakes Museum, 61–63, 66,
    78–79, 81–84, 90–91, 100, 101, 109–10,
    113–15
Dossin Maritime Group, 104
Douglas, Randi, *86*, 87
Dowling, Rev. Fr. Edward J., S.J., 62
Dressel, Barry, *68*, 81–82, 83, 84
Dressel, Judith, *68*
Duffield, Divie, 19, 27–28
Dunnigan, Brian Leigh, 100

Eaton, Gillian, *86*, 87
*Edmund Fitzgerald*, *88*, 90–91, 109
education programs, 38, 46, 72, 75, 91,
    100, 106, 113

financial crisis of 2008, 99–100
Finn, Albert, 27, 29
Finney, Jared, 29
Fitzsimmons, Percival, 35–36
Fort Wayne, 37, 48, 49–50, 77–79. *See also*
    Historic Fort Wayne
Frost, Bartlett, 55–56, *68*, 74

Given, C. J., 31
Glancy, Alfred R. Jr., 81, 129
Glancy Trains Exhibit, 81, 87, 93, 104, 129
Great Depression, 35–37, 48
Great Lakes Maritime Institute (GLMI),
    49, 90, 92, 104, 129–30
Greenstone, Ann, 105
Gregory, Amos, *67*
Gristmill Club, 31

Haggerty, T. J., 31
Hall, Kermit, 76
Hampton, Arthur, 31, 35–37, 38–39
Harvey, Howard I., 35

Hastings, Harold, 43, 74
Henry, David, 43
Hibbler, Dorothea, 77
Hickey, Edward, 66
Hill, Draper, 92
Historic Fort Wayne, 77–79, 81, 82, 85,
    103. *See also* Fort Wayne
Historic Memorials Society in Detroit
    (HMSD), 130
Historymobile, 75, 77, *86*
Holden, W. Sprague, 76
Hubbard, Julia, 38, 43

Indian-Pilgrim Dinner, 59, 60
International Shipmasters Association
    (ISMA), 83, 90, 130–31
Irwin, Tracy Smith, 101, 104

Jennings, Richard, 54
Jobagy, Beatrice, 74
Johnson, Arthur, 74
Jones, Robert, *86*, 87
*J. T. Wing*, 37, 48–49, 51, 60–61. *See also*
    Museum of Great Lakes History
Junior Benefit Committee, 105

Kapp, William, 42, 51, *52*, 61–62, 72
Kilpatrick, Kwame, 103
Kiskadden, Donald, 48, *52*, 65, 66
Kresge, Sebastian, 64–65, *67*
Kresge Educational Wing, 84
Kresge Exhibition Hall, 71, 72, 104
Kruckeberg, Vicky, 97
Krum, Gracie, 20, 27–28, 29, 31, 34, 37,
    39, 42, 46, 47, 60
Kukurugya, Stefan, *86*, 87
Kunz, Hazen, 66, *67*, *68*
Kuttruff, Karl, 78–79

Larson, Robert, 43, 47
Leadbetter, Thomas, 48, *68*, 74
lectures, 56–57
Lee, Robert, 56, 60, 62–64
Lost Mariners Remembrance, 119
Lyon, Maud Margaret, *69*, 73, 84, 91, 97,
    101

Marine Historical Society of Detroit
 (MHSD), 49, 131
Marsh, Florence, 37
Marx, Bud, 91
Mason, Philip, *68*, 74, 76
McConnell, Annette, 100
McConnell, Jim, 100
McGraw, Kathy, 130
McKaig, May, 44
McMillan, Mimi, *70*
McMillan, Sandy, *70*, 103, 105
McRae, Norman, 80
Mead, Hudson, 79
Memorandum of Understanding, 103–4
Metcalf, Mattie, 33
Michigan Council for the Arts and
 Cultural Affairs (MCACA), 72, 91, 96
Michigan Historical Society, 21
"Michigan in Perspective: Local History
 Conference," 57
Miller, Raymond, 37, 47, 50–51, 71, 75–76
Mills, Hazel (Mrs. Wilson W.), 43, *66*
*Miss Pepsi*, *89*, 90
Moran, J. Bell, 27, 28, 29, 31, 39, 50
Moross House, 77
Murphy, Mary (Mrs. Fred T.), 42, 48, *52*, 60
Murphy, Sarah, 115
Museum of Great Lakes History, 48–49,
 61. *See also* Dossin Great Lakes
 Museum; *J. T. Wing*

National Society of the Colonial Dames of
 America (NSCDA), 104, 131
Nauta, Patience, 80
Next Big Thing, The, 110
Nicholson, David, 105
Nolan, Barbara, 74
Norris, Joe, 37

Oral History Project, 121
Osen, Ken, 87

Palmer Log Cabin, 77
*Past>Forward* campaign, 105–6, 109, 110,
 *111*, *112*
Patriotic Award, 81
Patriot's Ball, 59

Pearsall, Margot, 56, 79
Pelham, Alfred, 66, 80
Penfield, Paul L., *67*
Peoples, John W., *68*
Perkins, Jim, *86*, 87
Phenix, William, 77, 87
photography, 113
Pierrot, George, 65
Pike, Francis, 42
*Pioneering*, 35
Polacsek, John, 82–83, 90
Pray, Carl E., 28
Prismatic Club of Detroit, 25
prohibition, 25

Quaife, Milo M., 59, 127

Rauhauser, Bill, 113
Rebellion, 71, 110
Reeves, Harry, 61
Replica Project, 35, 36–37
Rice, Gordon, 65, *67*
Riots, the, 71, 110
Risher, Jenny, 113
Robinson, E. Stephen, 90
Rudnick, Gregg, 130
Ruffner, Rick, *70*
Rugh, Elana, 115, 118
Ryding, Reuben, 57

Sadler, Bob, 100
Salminen-Witt, Rebecca, 115
Shattuck, Marquis, 74
Siebert, William, 28–29
Sillars, Mal, 91
Simons, Leonard, 43, 48, *52*, 66, *67*, *68*,
 75, 92
Slattery, Margaret, 66, 80
Smith (Irwin), Tracy, 101, 104
Smith, Mabel, 39
Smith, Mike, 92
social clubs, 25–26
social media, 115
sports clubs, 26
Stallworth, Alma, 79
Stark, George, 37, 39, 41–42, 47–48, 51,
 *52*, 62, 65, 66, *67*

Starr, Thomas, 39, 65
Stevens, Mark, 74
Stille, Glenn, 56, 74
Stocking, William, 27
StoryLiving, *86*, 87
Stoudamire, Marlowe, 110, 119
"Streets of Old Detroit," 54, *55*, 71, 100, 109
Strowger, Richard "Dick," *69*, 96, 100, 101

technology, 25, 91–92, 95
*Telescope* magazine, 130
Thompson, Ann, 79

Underground Railroad, 28–29

VanOotegham (Woodell), Michelle, 101
Vernor's 150th Anniversary Party, *108*, 115
Vinyard, JoEllen, 76
Voigt, Tobi, 110

Wayne State University, 37, 44, 46, 57
Weadock, Thomas, 35
Weeks, Patricia, 81
Weeks, Solon, *68*, 74–75, 79, 81

White, Josh Jr., *86*, 87
white flight, 76
Whittaker, Alfred, 48
Wilborn, Dave, *102*
Wilkinson, Warren, 84, 91
*William Clay Ford*, *89*, 90, 109
Williams House, 46
Winkleman, Beryl, *68*
Witkowski, Richard, 74
Women's Division, 34–35
Woodell, Michelle VanOotegham, 101
Woodford, Frank, 66, *68*
Wright, Robert, 56
Wright Museum of African American History, 71–72, 96
Wrigley, Barbara, 77, 80, 84
WWJ-AM, 75

Young, Cynthia, 77
youth program, 38, 113

Zembala, Ann, *70*
Zembala, Dennis, *70*, 100
Zieve, Mary Lou, *69*, 96